To Dad, Christmas 1986
From Pat & Chris.

A
NORFOLK
LOGBOOK

A
NORFOLK
LOGBOOK

**Keith Skipper
dips into
local waters**

© Keith Skipper 1986
Published by Keith Skipper and Jim Baldwin
Publishing, Fakenham.
Distributed to the trade by Paper-Klip
(Wholesale), Fakenham, Norfolk.
ISBN 0 948899 02 6

By The Same Author.
Dew Yew Keep 'a Troshin.
Down At The Datty Duck.
Dunt Fergit Ter Hevver Larf.
A Load Of Old Squit.

Front cover photo by Chris Durkin
Back cover photo via Brian Hedge

Typeset by Fakenham Photosetting Ltd.
Originated by Colourplan. Printed by Colour
Print and bound by Dickens Print Trade
Finishers.

A Product of Fakenham.

Foreword

It was, so I believe, the American actress Katharine Hepburn who was asked what she REALLY thought of things written about her in the newspapers.

"Darlings", she is reliably said to have replied ("darlings" being the obligatory password of Hollywood actresses of the day). "Darlings, I don't mind what they say, providing it isn't true."

The comment comes to mind after reading this manuscript because the tale seems to embrace the puzzlement which initially oozed into my consciousness. I had to face the fact, and still have to face it, that this is an extraordinary book. It is Skip at his most unusual and outrageous. It is Skip being serious, you see.

Consider for a moment. Those who have known and admired the art of Skipitis for many years will also know that, once started, it is notoriously difficult to stop. In recent years, to an extent, radio equipment manufacturers have sought to overcome the problem by supplying each set with an "off" switch, something more than one Norwich City manager and quite a few players would have liked to possess.

Even so, the flow of Skipspeak and Skipwrite, which once caused local newspaper readers to choke on their cornflakes, is now as familiar each dinnertime as indigestion. In other words, his removal from the world of the hack into the world of steam wireless has merely enabled enthusiasts to indulge at different mealtimes.

Yet none of this adequately explains the changes so glassily and magnificently apparent in these pages. We have still not answered the quantum leap question: why?

To attempt to find an answer an in-depth study of the phenomenon which is Keith is required. We need to search the pages of the book for clues. For example, what do Keith's own writings tell us about Skip the man?

Frankly, not a lot. He seems to be heavily into the lingo of natives and interested in the affairs of cottagers. He likes sugar beet and has a thing about

Jem Mace. He acknowledges the fact he is a media personality, yet professes to retain an interest in matters as elemental and humble as ploughing and cricket.

Clearly, what we are dealing with here is a multi-personality situation. Let me elucidate, spell out a few things the book does not tell you.

It hides the fact he once cracked a joke in the Carrow Road boardroom after a particularly heavy home defeat, and smoked far more than was good for him. It does not explain he was once without hair on the chin or describe what he looked like in those lean and pallid times. It makes no mention of how he once talked non-stop all the way from Norwich to Middlesbrough. And there is no word anywhere of the sadly lamentable state of his defensive play – regularly exploited by yours truly – at comb and penny football played on train compartment tables. As for the Alma Cogan fixation, the pages are blank. I can only hope there is another volume to come.

This is enough, I think, to show there are other sides to the man. What the individual reader makes of it all is up to the individual. But let me pose this question. Would you allow your daughter to lock herself in her bedroom to listen to the Dinnertime Show alone?

Summing up, I would say this is an innovative and towering book which clamours for attention. It is Skip at his most enigmatic and challenging. My own view, in seeking deeper meanings, is that he is actually trying to suggest that although Doris Day is unlikely to make a comeback we must never totally forget our debt to the past.

Enshrined within these pages may also be a first serious attempt to achieve wider literary acceptability; an early glimpse, in fact, of an infinitely more rounded image. If so, the private pocket book of merry Skip quips for all occasions could be a thing of the past.

A simplistic interpretation of his current work is that it is becoming increasingly and delightfully reflective. The theme of taking stock, introduced in the early chapters, runs ever stronger as reminiscences follow in eloquent and elegant sequence.

I think this could be Skip in the first blush of middle age. In any event, yer hev ter larf.

BRUCE ROBINSON
(Clement Court of the *Eastern Daily Press*)

Author's Thanks

Compiling a volume of this kind – bits and pieces from over the years – brings home the value of good friends and a useful storage system.

The last thing I threw away was a very weak line on the way back from a Norwich City match at Charlton. The first thing I did when planning this Norfolk Logbook was to call up old colleagues and friends to enlist their support. The threat of repeating that very weak line did the trick in some cases.

So much generosity and enthusiasm to throw light on the darker little corners of my memory and imagination. Some contribute words; others pass on pictures to do the talking. All do it willingly. Except those who may recall the journey home from Charlton.

Thanks to Clement Court of the *Eastern Daily Press* for his witty and revealing foreword. Enough there to prove he's a true Charlton supporter. In a previous life he was Bruce Robinson, a helpful colleague on the football reporting beat. The sound philosopher to my youthful extrovert. The well-organised essayist to my rather racy, pun-loving reporter. (I own up to "Hot Cross Bone Day" as the Canaries surged towards the First Division with some excellent Easter results, and ask for "Brum's Lullaby" to be taken into consideration.) Such a contrast, we enjoyed each other's company, and shared in Norfolk's delight as City went to Division One and Wembley for the first time.

From a Lincolnshire-born playboy to an international playwright. Arnold Wesker was quick to give me permission to use his crop of "Sugar Beet", knocked and topped when he was in Norfolk over thirty years ago. I'm sure that reflects his deep affection for the county and its people – as well as betraying misguided faith in a native so eager to give his work a fresh coat of the vernacular!

John Kett's delightful dialect poem "Harry The Hossman" brooks no interference, and goes perfectly in harness with the pictures and yarns extolling the splendours of horses on the land.

Alan Howard's pictorial peep at Ron Saunders' reign as Carrow Road king underlines the sharpness of the medicine dispensed on the Mousehold training beat. John Marr's selection from the local cricket scene captures a growing competitive edge to the summer game. Les Gould reminds us just in time that we all need a good laugh to help keep the sporting world in perspective.

Perhaps it's more significant than we realise that so many showbusiness personalities use sport as an antidote to the pressures of their calling. Mind you, how would Max Bygraves cope with a five-day Test at Old Trafford, or Jimmy Tarbuck square up to the challenge of being player-manager at Anfield?

My warmest thanks also to Clifford Temple and Brian Hedge for their photographic support, along with all others happy to illustrate a co-operative streak. A special salute towards Eastern Counties Newspapers for such ready permission to quote from articles and reproduce pictures from their files. Some of the material goes beyond my 17-year connection with the firm – both before and since – and that suggests someone remembers me buying a round long after "Hot Cross Bone Day" was ticked off at Prospect House.

Finally, thanks to Norfolk for keeping still often enough for me to take notice since I hastened the end of the war by being born in 1944.

Keith Skipper

Dark Mutterings

I accepted more than a week ago that parochialism no longer fills up your glass at sherry parties, or even stamps a passport into polite society. The novelty value of Norfolk natives seems to be wearing thin.

In fact, we're harassed rather than heralded in some quarters. Not simply labelled a piffling prophet without honour in his own county, but dismissed as an anachronism in the latter part of the 20th century.

"So you're a local broadcaster and scribbler? But don't you have a real job as well? Oh, you try to keep the local dialect alive, and you don't like some of the things happening to Norfolk ... Jolly good! Someone has to keep us in order! Have you tried Fleet Street or Panorama? Pass the olives, there's a good chap."

They've got you sorted out. Norfolk-lover is a euphemism for stick-in-the-mud, a pedlar in nostalgia, a narrow-minded refugee from Parishpumpland, a cold left-over from an idyllic pastoral scene. There might be time to humour you, and say it's nice to see people building their own village halls and reviving the old-fashioned community spirit. The art of condescension is not dead. But you get no more than a crash course in harsh economics when you mention disappearing pubs, schools, buses and hedgerows.

Bringing you to the boil is easy. Watching you let off steam has its hazards. Champions of the vernacular have a disarming habit of bringing it into play to confuse or confound the opposition.

Many a scullery maid has cursed a dowager and lived to savour the tale. The odd serf must have damned his feudal landlord and been allowed to keep his chains. Dark mutterings in dialect have been interpreted by new village parsons as welcome signs of repentance among the congregation. School-teachers are not immune; I heard of one who gave a pupil a housemark after being informed that "Yew duzzy ole fewl!" was a pre-Chaucer greeting.

Swearing in broad Norfolk carries an almost lyrical ring. And if you smile when you do it, chances are the target will consider it some kind of ancient

"You can always tell a Norfolk man ... but you can't tell him much!" Keith Skipper, pitchforked to stardom in "Mother Goose", the 1982 panto at Norwich Theatre Royal, takes on the formidable Nora Batty with a bit of rustic backchat.

blessing. Remember, too, that ethnic minorities have quaint little ways to go with the words.

Just watch the old regular down at the local pub get his message across to the new, keen landlord who has to be trained quickly in local customs. The cap is slowly pushed back, and a gnarled finger and thumb pinch the lined forehead until it hurts. The old boy chunters into his glass as if in rustic prayer.

"Woss the bottum dropt owt? Look lyke rearn ... but thass gittin on fer nearly kwid a pynt. Woss the brarry runnin' short, ole partner? Iyre bin a' cummin heer fer thatty nyne yeer. Could git ter lyke it..."

As the voice trails away, the glass, magically, is brimmed to the top. The new landlord may not have understood much of the gentle tirade, but he got the gist – the beer facts. The old customer has converted steam into an art form with a strange, subtle, native cunning.

Fear of the unknown, or of the incomprehensible, will continue to hound newcomers to Norfolk. However, before we can settle down for a good, clean fight in an ever-changing world, there are traitors to be rooted out and brought to justice. These are the ones who really bring me to the boil. Sons and daughters of Norfolk who are ashamed of their calling. They're not so much letting the side down as asking for the game to be abandoned. Trying to crack their jaw, and pretending they've left their copy of *Burke's Peerage* at home.

A telephone voice is one thing: cheating in public is another. Nor is intelligent company likely to be fooled or impressed by verbal fumbling. Mrs Malaprop never could sound like Malcolm Muggeridge. We have all been uneasy in certain company. My early days as a reporter on the local newspapers were littered with potentially embarrassing moments at important funerals, big meetings and posh presentations. It took bravado allied to a sense of humour to ask if it was all right to park my landlady's bike outside near the Bentley, and then admit you'd rather have a half of bitter than a glass of whatever the rest of the cast were sipping.

There were times when the words "Local Press" had to be hurled high above the hubbub to get any attention, but I soon discovered that being yourself forestalled or at least minimised the risk of being either pitied or patronised. I'll agree that a reporter can find it easier to earn swift acceptance. After all, he's usually there to offer something few people can resist – free publicity. (Although there were occasions at local magistrates courts when the recipients didn't seem to be all that grateful!)

Since the arrival of BBC Radio Norfolk in 1980, I've had a privileged position to sing the county's praises or, when appropriate, to criticise. I made 1982 "NDP Year". Nothing to do with politics ... simply Norfolk Dialect Preservation. Short stories with local flavour, letters written completely in dialect and countless limericks using Norfolk place names or expressions underlined the amount of backing for that little project.

There were a few complaints, usually from anonymous callers who resented the idea of their children being subjected to such hideous words as "gut-eark" and "troshin'". And on the BBC as well! Little point in starting a debate on humour or heritage after giving such offence, so I consoled myself with droll epistles from self-confessed foreigners who said they were working hard to learn a new language.

One woman on holiday from Blackburn did get her own back by filling up three sheets of paper with a choice selection of her native phrases, posted from "somewhere on the Broads". I did the honourable thing – and asked BBC Radio Lancashire for an interpreter to put me fully in the picture. Paraphrased, the message was something like: "Wish you were here."

With local radio still comparatively young in this area, the sound of pure, undiluted Norfolk coming over the airwaves continues to make a big impact. "Blarst, thass whooly good ter hear it, bor!" One of the blessings must be the alternative to "Mummerzet" accents to which we have been subjected by the national networks, wireless and television for so many years.

They say it's one of the hardest dialects to do properly, however talented the performer, and I recall falling about in disbelief at the mock Norfolk tones of the "locals" in that BBC TV soap opera about an overspill town, "The Newcomers", a few years back. It seemed that a drawn-out "aaah!", a cloth cap and a piece of string had to cover a multitude of misguided handbooks on rustic tones.

When I first met playwright Arnold Wesker, he agreed that the accent was mighty hard to capture, both on paper and on stage, but a production of his "Roots" at the Maddermarket Theatre in Norwich was one of the best, simply because the players had authentic voices. And if the voices are right, surely everything else is that much more credible?

I'm proud of my Norfolk pedigree, and have no qualms about employing the vernacular if the occasion demands, on or off the air. It has a rich seam of humour always ready to be tapped, although I get annoyed when it is adopted – or stolen – by visiting after-dinner speakers in the hope of ingratiating themselves with the peasantry or getting away with a downright crude story. That makes a mockery of its true value.

There is an ambivalent attitude in many quarters towards local accents. "It's quaint, worth preserving and stops us from all being the same" they say – and then accuse you of putting it on in the hope of currying favour with people who think it's quaint, worth preserving and stops us from all being the same....

Then there are surveys designed to keep the old pot boiling. "Many people in Britain put their foot in it as soon as they open their mouths...judgement of character by accent is growing rather than diminishing ... people who speak the Queen's English, technically known as Received Pronunciation, are considered to possess qualities like honesty, integrity, intelligence, ambition or even good looks." Professor John Honey, of Leicester University, gave us those little gems a couple of years ago. Someone from Norfolk must have told him that the whole business becomes totally confusing when the Royal Family and old Harry up the road both say "orf" for "off" and "lorst" for "lost".

In recent years, I've had the pleasure of adjudicating at the special evening set aside for Norfolk dialect enthusiasts at the Cromer and North Norfolk Festival of Music and Drama. Familiar voices raising a defiant chorus in the face of growing demands for dull uniformity.

There's an element of cheerful competition, and there may be a drop of self-indulgence. Even so, it's rare for a "serious" festival in these parts to find a place for a prolonged hymn of praise to the dialect. I think the BBC and ITV should sponsor the evening, if only to remind them of that genuine article so often missing when they use a Norfolk setting for a production to be seen and heard nationwide.

One sad note struck at Cromer each year is the shortage of youngsters either willing or able to take part. I've heard various reasons put forward as to why a precious tradition is being left almost exclusively to older tongues, not just on this local stage but right across the county. Many children think it's cissy, even a cause for shame, to speak with a Norfolk accent, and the last thing they want to do is risk even more ridicule by putting it on public display.

It's hardly accepted, let alone encouraged, in local schools these days. Many of the teachers have come from other areas, and so have a fair percentage of the pupils, and that's added to the pressures on Norfolk-born youngsters. At best they're "quaint"; at worst, they're "thick", and made to feel embarrassed for daring to do in class what comes quite naturally at home and at play.

I'm sure there are some enlightened teachers, proud of their own roots cultivated in Birmingham, Scotland, London or Cardiff, and they bring a degree of tolerance to a difficult area of debate. Perhaps they are able to stand Chaucer alongside the Boy John, or Arnold Wesker next to Robert Forby and his Vocabulary of East Anglia.

But when it becomes apparent that those with a flair and a feeling for the local vernacular are being relegated to an ethnic minority in their own county, it must be time to be blatantly parochial. Dilution may be inevitable, but that can't mean any dialect should simply be allowed to curl up and die. Values here can't be measured in tangible ways. One person's individual quirk is another's abiding passion. For some, the beauty of dialect is the study of its derivations. For others, it beams through the humour of its hand-me-down stories.

I see it as a vital expression of individualism at a time when so many smothering influences are at work, like a big, wet blanket over any pocket of non-conformity. "Dewin' diffrunt" must be more than a neat little motto for Norfolk.

Holding Hands

Norfolk humour and the Norfolk dialect hold hands like inseparable lovers. You can't have one without the other, although some of the yarns supposed to be indigenous to these parts are well-travelled vehicles of amusement given a local coat of paint.

Yes, there's an earthy flavour to many of the stories – a legacy, no doubt, of being so close to nature out in the sticks – but the recurring themes are to do with an inherent dislike of pomposity and an admiration for the rustic underdog who has the last bark.

There's also a strange kind of perverted logic about our humour:

"Where are yew gowin, Harry bor?"

"I ent gowin nowheer – Iym just cummin back!"

☆   ☆   ☆   ☆

I see m'ole mearte Fred leanin' up ginst the gearte, wi' this gret ole alsearshun dawg asyde onnim.

"Wotcher, Fred. Dew yar dawg bite?"

"No."

I lean down, and this dawg tearke whool sleeve owter my jackit.

"Blarst, thowt yew sed yar dawg dunt bite....!"

"That ent my dawg."

☆   ☆   ☆   ☆

Norfolk sage: "Live each day as if thass yer larst – an' wun day yew'll be rite!"

☆   ☆   ☆   ☆

◄ *"Now howld yow hard tergather!" Sidney Grapes points to rustic harmony.*

Of course, countless little philosophical gems have lit up our rustic humour over the years. Perhaps the most durable came from Sidney Grapes in his "Boy John" letters to the *Eastern Daily Press* between 1946 and 1958. The sayings of Aunt Agatha, enshrined as postscripts, are still quoted freely and finding new targets ... "Aunt Agatha she say if yew want to keep friends wi' the peeple in yar willage, keep orf the parish council", and "Aunt Agatha she say thass a pity we carnt live in the past – it would be so much cheaper", are good examples.

Sidney Grapes lived all his life in the Broadland village of Potter Heigham. He enjoyed local fame for many years as a Norfolk comedian at concerts and dinners before he wrote the first "Boy John" letters and introduced Granfar, Aunt Agatha and the cantankerous old Mrs W—. The letters remain a delightful microcosm of Norfolk country life after the war, full of wry humour, topical satire and droll accounts of village events and characters.

Born in 1888, Sidney spoke a brand of dialect that hadn't been diluted by "foreign" influences. It was said he wrote as he spoke and spelt as he pleased. On stage, he played the rustic who wasn't such a fool as he might have looked – and you had to be a Norfolk man like him to join in the rustic triumph at the end of the story. The rugged, humorous face under the old "chummy" hat. The wagging finger. "Now howld yow hard tergather!" The audience invariably finished up laughing with him, and there was no room for malice in such togetherness.

Jonathan Mardle, in his tribute to Sidney Grapes, "Humorist and Philosopher", wrote: "It is not always true of popular writers that they are personally worthy of the affection inspired by the characters they invent. But Sidney Grapes, as a man, was altogether worthy of the affection that the Boy John engendered in his readers." Evidently, Sidney's listeners found his concert turns just as endearing. The word "kind" is used just as much as "funny" among those fortunate enough to have enjoyed his company.

"You can allus tell a Norfolk man – but yew carnt tell 'im much!" That seems as good a text as any with which to introduce a selection of Norfolk stories that, for me, capture the character and spirit of the place.

☆   ☆   ☆   ☆

An elderly lady was interviewing a young Norfolk girl with a view to employing her as a domestic servant.

"Well, Audrey, I think you will suit me very well, provided you always remember I am a lady of few words. So if I beckon to you like this, you will know that I mean 'Come here'."

"Thass orrite, mum," replied Audrey cheerfully. "An if I shearke my hid lyke this heer, yewll know I arnt a' cummun!"

☆   ☆   ☆   ☆

The sergeant was parading the raw recruits for the first time, and had picked out Thompson, a tall Norfolk lad, for the Right Marker – that's the poor fool who stands alone at the end of the front rank. The sergeant managed to line them up, turn them right and start them marching, but on his command "Halt!" they all stopped except Thompson. He carried on, swinging both arms at once.

"What's your bloody game, laddie ... are you deaf?" roared the sergeant.

"I ent deaf. I kin hear yew. But I just carnt git ewsed tew it yit."

"So ... we've managed to find another swedebasher, have we? Let's have another little go."

He sorted them out, lined them up and marked them off again. The sergeant let them go for a bit and then shouted:

"Platoon, Halt! Thompson ... WHOA!"

☆　　☆　　☆　　☆

The farmworkers started at 6.30 a.m. They lived in cottages on the farm and went home to breakfast. One of the old boys married, but he didn't know that the woman he wed didn't like getting up in the mornings. Well, he got fed up with coming home for breakfast only to find a cold kitchen and no food. One cold, wet morning he was feeling really miserable. He looked up and saw smoke coming from all the other chimneys.

He rushed into his house and shouted up the stairs: "Fire! Fire!" His wife sprang out of bed, came thumping down the stairs shouting:

"Where? Where?" He looked her straight in the eye.

"In everybody else's house bar ours!"

☆　　☆　　☆　　☆

The village know-all was looking over the hedge as old George was digging up his potatoes.

"Cor, they're little ole things ter year, arnt ther?"

"So they might be – but I grow 'em ter fit my mouth, nut yors!"

☆　　☆　　☆　　☆

A Norfolk man on top of a stack shouted to his mate: Horry, jist yew cum up heer a minnit an lissun." Horry climbed the ladder, and after a minute or so said: "I carnt heer noffin."

"No," said his mate. "Ent that whooly quiet."

☆　　☆　　☆　　☆

Sidney Grapes in his washerwoman outfit as he entertains some good old Norfolk boys.

BELOW: "Yew kin orl joyn in the chorus — an less be hearin' on yer at the back!"

Old George went up to London for the first time, and he tells his friends all about it on his return to the village pub: "I git orf the tewb an start walkin' down Orxford Street. They wuz orl gorn ser farst, bor, an afore I knew it, I wuz runnin' anorl – an' I wunt gorn nowheer!"

☆   ☆   ☆   ☆

This woman always clung to her sheets in the morning. Her long-suffering husband took up her usual cup of tea and told her she was missing all the lovely sunrises.

"Dunno why yew keep gorn on bowt it . . . thass oonly a bludder sunset gorn backerds!"

☆   ☆   ☆   ☆

Two rural sages were discussing the merits or otherwise of making the A11 a dual carriageway.

"Carnt see ner sense innit mesself; cor blarst, there'll be thowsunds onnem hossin itter Norfolk. Weel be wyde opin cors thatell be eesier ter git heer . . .

The other chap thought for a minute. Then he beamed: Ah, so that myte – but that mean they'll cleer orf quicker anorl!"

☆   ☆   ☆   ☆

A Norfolk girl went to London to be a nanny to a rather posh family, and then turned on the airs and graces when she came back to see her parents. She convinced them they ought to move into a better house.

Mother saw an advert for one she liked, and asked her "bigoty" daughter what "terraced" meant.

"Oh," she purred. "That means it's semi-detached on both sides."

☆   ☆   ☆   ☆

It was time for the Nativity Play in a Norfolk village school. Mary and Joseph saluted the arrival of Baby Jesus, folded him carefully in teacher's shawl and placed him lovingly in the plant pot trough serving as a crib.

Joseph asked if the boy was behaving himself – and that was the cue for Mary to show her ad-libbing skill.

"He ent ser bad darrin' the day, but hees a littel sod at nites!"

☆   ☆   ☆   ☆

The daughter was just leaving after paying her regular Friday night call on her aged father.

"Look after yourself, and have a nice weekend," she called.

He scowled and groaned: "Freard Iyre med uther plans."

☆   ☆   ☆   ☆

A small boy turned up at the village shop just before closing time on a Saturday evening. "Toylet rowl, pleese mister."

The shopkeeper took one from the shelf and handed it over. First thing Monday morning, the boy was back as the door was unlocked. He had the toilet roll under his arm. He strode to the counter and thrust the item towards the shopkeeper:

"Mum say kin yew tearke it back – cumpany dint cum!"

☆   ☆   ☆   ☆

Some youngsters were conducting a funeral service in the back garden for their recently-demised guinea pig. As they lowered him into his final resting place, one of them said solemnly:

"In the nearmer the Farther, the Son – in the whool he goest. Owrmin."

☆   ☆   ☆   ☆

Two Norfolk lads were doing their Christmas Eve shopping in Norwich. Both were heavily laden with gifts as they met on the market:

"Hullo Passy bor. Yewre dewin well. Yew ent brook yit?"

"No Harbert – but Iym gittin whooly bent!"

☆   ☆   ☆   ☆

Jacob was twelve and "backus boy" at the Squire's. That meant he did all the dirty, unpleasant little jobs, like cleaning boots and carrying the coals, or anything else the maid was too high-minded to do. One day, Squire came into the yard where Jacob was chopping kindling, and handed him a hare he'd just shot.

"Take that to the Rectory, boy, and be quick about it!"

Now, the Rector was noted for being mean, and Jacob was in no mood to trudge the mile to the Rectory with a heavy hare, for he was hoping to get a game on the village green before it was dark. He muttered to himself as he went, dragging the hare behind him: "Gotter tearke this bludder ole hare ter the Parsun, and he oont gi' me noffin."

Jacob expected to see the maid when he knocked on the back door, so he said in surly tones: "Squire sear Iyre gotter gi' yew this." To his surprise, it was the Rector who opened the door.

"Now Jacob," he said reproachfully. "That's not the way to present a gift. I'll show you how to do it correctly. Give me the hare. I'll knock on the door and you open it."

So he knocked on the door and when Jacob opened it, the Rector said: "Please sir, Squire sends you this and hopes you will kindly accept it."

Jacob replied with a grin: "Thankyer moi littel man – an' heer's harf a crown fer yar trubble!"

☆   ☆   ☆   ☆

It was the day of the funeral for a woman who'd been thoroughly disliked in the village. She'd henpecked her husband, driven her children mercilessly and picked arguments with all the neighbours. It was very overcast, and as the service ended a violent storm broke. There was a blinding flash of lightning, followed by a terrific clap of thunder.

"Blarst me," says Old Billy. "Dint tearke har long ter git there!"

☆   ☆   ☆   ☆

Members of the village darts team decided to go carol singing on Christmas Eve in aid of local charities. They worked out the programme: do the middle of the village in the early evening, call at the pub for some refreshments, proceed to the Hall and then on to Primrose Farm.

They were on schedule when they got to the Hall, but liberal hospitality meant it was almost midnight and very dark as they left for Primrose Farm. When they arrived, it seemed all inmates had retired. All was quiet.

They sang, "Christians Awake!" and "While Shepherds Watched". No lights came on, but there were strange sounds coming from the place. The leader decided to take a closer look. He returned.

"Dew yew lissun heer tergather. Better keep yar gobs shut in the willuj. Weer jist bin a' singin tew the cowshud!"

☆   ☆   ☆   ☆

P.S. Granfar he say – If wimmun know ser much, how cum they arsk ser menny questyuns?

Sugar Beet

Arnold Wesker put Norfolk on an international stage with "Roots". On Tuesday, October 2nd, 1984, I helped repay the compliment by organising the world premiere of something he wrote over thirty years earlier while working in the county.

"Sugar Beet" is a dialogue between two farm workers as they put their backs into it up and down the rows. Wesker wrote it in 1953, and claims it was turned down by the *Eastern Daily Press*! I thought it worthy of a wider audience although the agricultural scene it depicts has long since disappeared.

The world-famous playwright was back in the area for a special week of events initiated by BBC Radio Norfolk, thanks, in many respects, to Wesker's friendship with our then news editor, Ian Hyams. It was on the station's Dinnertime Show that I chatted to the writer about his work – and gave a world premiere to "Sugar Beet".

Wesker did the scene-setting, while his nephew, Keith Keeble, and I had the starring roles. There had been time for only a couple of rehearsals in the Radio Norfolk kitchen, appropriately enough. The evening before we had joined the author and his wife Dusty, from Starston, for a production of "The Kitchen" at The Maddermarket Theatre, in Norwich. That play has its roots in Wesker's experiences at the city's Bell Hotel and at other restaurants in London and Paris.

"The world might have been a stage for Shakespeare, but to me it is a kitchen," he said. The underlying theme is work, with its turmoils and petty squabbles, the sacrifice of quality to quantity, the overbearing hierarchy. The play makes big demands of designer, stage manager, director and players, but Wesker was impressed with the Maddermarket production.

He was quite pleased with our treatment of "Sugar Beet", and didn't mind that I'd taken several liberties with the script he'd put together in 1953.

In fact, he gave me permission to make any more amendments I pleased,

◀ *The sugar beet harvest is hard on the back muscles. The old-fashioned way at Bawburgh.*
(Picture by Clifford Temple.)

and to publish it in this volume devoted to all things Norfolk. Wesker's work – Skipper's parochial touches!

That successful week of events staged in his honour, winding up with a literary lunch at the Maddermarket, revived some of the arguments provoked by the first production of his play "Roots".

"This is a play about Norfolk people: it could be a play about any country people and the moral could certainly extend to the metropolis." Despite those words in his preamble to the play and his determination to get the local dialect right – embers of anger are still aglow in some quarters.

Wesker remains surprised and saddened at any suggestion that his aims embraced a belittling of the sort of people he portrayed. He didn't draw a romantic, pastoral picture with stock-in-trade rustics catching their smocks on the brambles and finding inner strength through constant communion with Mother Nature.

There is comedy in "Roots", perhaps much of it inherent in the way Norfolk natives describe their ailments, but there's none of the saucy satire you can find, for instance, in a classic like "Cold Comfort Farm".

Wesker doesn't go along with my reading of the play, but he says others have been even wider of the mark! For me, "Roots" emphasises the stark restraints of a rural straitjacket, both on those who are unaware of being held down and the more "enlightened" characters who want to build bridges and escape from the third-rate.

The drama's central character, Beattie Bryant, finds a new sense of awareness through her boyfriend in London, and battles to convince her family they can break out as well. She's articulate and free at the end. They will continue to live as before.

Hardly a flattering assessment of Norfolk country life, and I wonder what they made of it when it was first presented at the Belgrade Theatre in Coventry in May, 1959. Another intriguing question: what sort of reception would it have got had it opened in Norwich instead?

I can provide a few little pointers based on classroom reaction when we read and talked about it at Hamond's Grammar School in Swaffham in my sixth-form days.

The fact that Norfolk had been put on a national stage by a serious playwright who'd lived and worked here prompted murmurs of approval. We'd had enough of the "village idiot" comic cuts with a Mummerzet accent. But what about this warts-and-all treatment for characters so close to home?

Remember, many of my colleagues also hailed from what the town boys liked to call "cow-muck and sugar beet land". There was some safety in numbers, and we shared a healthy sense of Norfolk humour. But "Roots" still managed to expose some tender spots.

I suspect we were over-sensitive in our youthful contributions to the great debate, especially when a master claimed that country lads receiving a good education could easily fall foul of "cultural snobbery". You know, being ashamed of parents because they hadn't discovered the wonders of Shakespeare, D. H. Lawrence – or even Arnold Wesker.

Even so, the collective answer was one I stored away for regular use in the years to follow. It's so tempting to be pompous about "escaping" from a rural background, and "getting on in the world". We Norfolk schoolboys of 25 years ago saluted Wesker's portrayal as an honest and timely contribution to arguments about a situation that had as much to do with lack of opportunity as it did with ignorance or insensitivity.

Our good fortune in having the chance to build bridges did not presume a slap in the face for those who'd worked so hard to provide us with the materials. That's not simple rustic loyalty. That's simple gratitude. And it doesn't date.

I've changed along with Norfolk, but I've stayed here with my family roots. When Wesker returned to the county which has inspired a fair amount of his output, I relished the chance to continue that mardle he started in a Swaffham classroom.

No doubt he started fresh ones on his visits to local schools. He certainly raised laughs at that literary lunch held in his honour when he revealed there had been suspicions he was a spy for the Russians. On his departure from The Bell in Norwich thirty years ago, local detectives swooped to interview every member of staff about the kitchen porter and his girl friend – and hinted darkly that he'd been a spy in the pay of Russian intelligence. No-one interviewed Wesker on the matter.

As he left this time, he described Norwich as "the one city outside London for which I feel the most affectionate, grateful and tender feelings, for giving me my earliest play – and my only wife".

He gave me this country dialogue as a memento. I pass it on, with phonetic liberties taken, as a tribute to those who have experienced the rigours of knockin' and toppin':

☆   ☆   ☆   ☆

"Sheez knockin' well terday."
"Yeh. Wunt werry wet overnoyte, wuz it?"
"No. Look lyke thass gorter be fair owd day."
"Yeh. Them beet 'er droy ter mornin'."
"They are anorl. Knock easy, dunt ther?"
"Yeh. Dunt dew ter hev it tew wet overnoyte, dew it? Tew hevvy."
"Big tew, arnt ther?"
"Yeh."
"Mearke hevvy gowin when that owd mowld cling ter' it."
"Yeh ... dunt dew ter hev 'em tew hevvy orl day. Ruff on th'owd rists."
"Yeh."
"But thass good job terday. Mowld forl orff easy. Iyre known this fild when

International play-wright Arnold Wesker discusses the script of "Sugar Beet" with Keith Skipper before the world premiere on BBC Radio Norfolk.
(Picture by Alan Howard.)

that wuz shin deep in mud. Shin deep, I tellyer. An we hatter push th' owd cart anorl cors the tractor got stuck."

"Yeh."

"Yeh. An theyre hed frorst onnem tew."

"But sheez knockin' orrite terday."

The seven o'clock sun came up red over the huge, flat field of green beet as the two men bent down again to the next row.

"Member that Lunnuner wot wakked heer larst yeer?"

"That wuz afore my tyme, wunt it?"

"When'd yew cum then?"

"March o' this yeer."

"Just afore yor tyme, then. He wuz heer three munth afore Chrismuss. Yeh. Dint stay ner longer. Hed nuff arter fast cupple daze on sugarbeet."

"Yeh?"

"Yeh. He say ter owd Buckley, he say, 'Blarst, this ent ner test fer manhood – this heer's test fer insannerty!' An owd Buckley he say ter this heer chap, he say, 'Yew better pack up then.' An he say, 'Yeh, rekun Iyd better.' He dint larst long! Kweer sorter chap he wuz. He say ter me, he say, 'Dunt they hev mershines ter dew this heer job?' An I say they hev mershines orrite, but that wunt dew fer Buckley ter hev enny cors he wunt want nunner us then."

"No, that he wunt, thass trew nuff. Hevver mershine fer the beet, an Buckley wunt hev us go arter 'em in the winter. Heel send us arter the barley, an thass the lot fer us fer the yeer."

"I tell him that."

"Wod he say then?"

"Huh! He dunt say noffin; he jist puller fearse an carry on arter the beet, an I arsk him when he git hoom, is he gorter dew enny gardnin'!"

"An wod he say ter that?"

"He dunt rekun thass funny, cors he say, 'We hent gotter garden!'"

The long rows of beet leaves shook in the wind and the piles of knocked beet lay neatly rowed, ready for topping; pale lines along the brown earth. Somewhere over the morning the eight-ten train hummed, and fifty minutes later the nine o' clock train hooted by, and the two men stopped for tea and thick sandwiches.

"Thass fair owd job this weather. Buckley rekun weer gorter hev Indyan summer."

"No tellin' is theer?"

"No, theer ent."

◀ *A breather for five lads at Calthorpe, during the 1950s. They are, left to right: Titch Lambert, Joe Flowerdew, Jack Goodwin, Stanley Norman and Pat Dennis. Stanley Norman, who provided the picture – says: "The crop was 21 tons. 6 cwt. We got £6 per acre, plus 1/3d per ton. Three of us pulled 65 acres and topped them. We carted them at £4 per acre, loading by hand. My hand didn't shake when I took my money."*

"Wot wuz that Lunnuner dewin down heer, then?"

"Cum ter wakk on the land, he say. He hev sum fun gorn arter the harvist, but sewns ever he start on the beet, blarst he hed enuff!"

"Yeh?"

"Yeh. He finished up so he wuz on orl fours. 'Back-brearkin', barstard job!' he say. 'Back-brearkin', hart-brearkin' an sowl-destroyin'!' he say. They wuz his wads. Heed start fresh in the mornin' an carry on till bowt levun ... then he start slowin' up. Iyd be way ahid o' him, an' I hatter stop so heed ketch up. 'Sheez a back-earkin' owd job' I say. 'She bludder is!' he say. 'She bludder is!' I tell him streart ... we wunt dew 't less we wuz forced tew. No moor we wunt, wood we?"

"No, bor, that we wunt. Wass tymer the yeer, I rekun, Ent no wasser tymer yeer fer gorn arter the beet when yer hans is tew frooz ter howld them leaves."

"No ... an I towld 'im that anorl."

"Wod he say?"

"He say suffin bowt bein' ortermaytun."

"Woss wunner them, then?"

"He say thass merkanical hoss or suffin ... an, by Christ, he needed wunner them tyme heed un that day!"

"Bet he lyked Lunnun arter that!"

"Yeh... They ent ewsed ter it, yer know. They dunt know wot hard wakk is up Lunnun."

Somewhere in the clear autumn sky two jet planes chased and wooed each other, scattering the surprised but patient birds out of their tree-top nests. From the distance came the slow sound of a tractor bringing the cart and more men to top and take away the knocked beet. A third of the large field was brown now; a trampled, muddy shore bordering the sodden, sea-green beet. The two soaked men stood a minute in front of the new row and surveyed what they had done and what they would do.

"Thass the tew-earker dun now, ent it?"

"Yeh. An weel be up this heer row an' down the nixt afore dinner tyme."

"Yeh."

"Ewsed only ter dew row an' harf longer him, thow. Wunce, we took tew howr ter dew wun row, an at ender that he say, 'Iym finishin' arter this row. Buckley kin tearke tyme orff mer pay.' I say ter him, 'Yew unt ever git ewsed tew 't if yer give up.' He say, 'Iyll git ewsed tew 't ... in smorl doses. But Iyre hed nuff fer terday,' he say. 'Woss matter, bor?' I say. He say, 'I ent no ewse ter yew, slowin' yew up. That wearste farmer's tyme anorl, an I wunt ber ner ewse ter mesself afore long,' he say. 'Yew dunt wotter worry bowt me, ole partner,' I say ter him. 'Cors Iyll go farster an yew. Stand ter reesun. Iym moor ewsed tew 't an wot yew are, boy. Wuh, me bein sixter an yew twetty dunt mearke ner diffrense,' I say. 'Yew dunt wotter tearke ner notiser me; if I go kwicker 'n' yew, blarst, thass only nattrel.' He wuz on orl fours on the grownd he wuz.

Coont move. He keep gitting up, yer see. Well, that dunt dew ner good ter keep gitting up, dew 't?"

"No, that dunt ... no, that dunt."

"An I tell him that anorl. I say, 'Yew dunt wotter keep gittin up. I know yew wont tew sumtymes. We orl dew. Blarst, nun onnus kin keep gorn wi' owt gitting up now an agin. An nor we carnt, kin we?' But yew ... yew stand up every minnit!' I say. 'Yew dunt wotter dew that; that dunt mearke yer feel ner better forrit. Thass rum job I know ter stay down when yer wotter git up. But yew keep gowin, ole partner, jist yew keep gowin. Yewll git ewsed tew 't. Yewll git ser ewsed tew't, yew wunt notise noffin,' I say ter him."

"Dew he pack up, then?"

"No, he dint. We hev howr left an he pick hisself up an puller fearse an carry streart on. Ryte slow, mynd yer. But he go on fer bowt twetty minnit. He stop ... but he dunt lift his back. Nut wunce. He leen on his knees and he sit on his hornshes wi' his back bent, or he jist stop and dunt knock. But fer bowt twetty minnit he jist dint lift his back. Then he stop harfway up the row an he sit down on that muck and he look sorter sad. Then he git up agin, and start hittin them bloomin beet ser hard! Blarst me, wunce he miss an knock hisself cleen orf his feet! Cum fourer clock he look fit ter drop."

"Ennywun else wiyyer?"

"Theer wuz him and me knockin ... and Harry, Jarge, Willy an' Monty toppin. When we wuz dun, owld Monty, he cum ter this heer chap and he say ter him, 'Blarst me! Yew looks thow yewre hed nuff fer the day!' An he say, 'Yeh, rekun I hev!' And Monty, he say ter him, 'Wot yew want now is ter tearke yew a mawther, bowt sixteen er seventeen ... thass what yew want now.' This yung feller, he say, 'That seem ter me thass yor remerdee fer evrathing rownd heer!' And Monty, he say, 'So that is, bor ... so that is!' He say, 'Yew wotter tearke har till har heerpins stand on ind!' Heez rum lad, owld Monty. He go arter the bit when he want tew, dunt he?"

"Yeh."

"Yeh."

A dog sniffed in crazy circles after what he thought was a rabbit, and the dull thud, thud, thud of the earth being knocked off the beet was a continual background rhythm to the flat land's quiet noises. The air was heavy with late warmth.

"Wotter be lyke this heer orl the tyme, dunt it?"

"Yeh. Fair owd job, this heer."

"Yeh. Go on orl day lyke this."

"Yeh ..."

"Yeh ..."

It was a rich and satisfied Norfolk countryside, worked and worn. And where the earth had already been ploughed up after the harvest, it seemed as if the land were yawning, very, very tired.

Hard Man

Ron Saunders took Norwich City's footballers to Division One for the first time. He also paved the way to Wembley with his own brand of true grit fashioned on the slopes of Mousehold. A disciplinarian, who regarded briar patches as inevitable before you could get to the roses. He arrived at Carrow Road in the summer of 1969, the Canaries' tenth manager since the war. In three seasons, he transformed a club with a Second Division complex into Championship material.

Cornerstone of that drive was a belief that piles of graft could compensate for any limitations in skill. Sweat and dedication to plug those gaps instead of the cheque-book some of his predecessors banked on for survival as much as star-gazing.

It wasn't long before Saunders was marching his troops up and down the slopes of Mousehold. He made players proud of not being sick on the first day back after a spot of good living during the summer. He referred constantly to the need for them to go through the pain barrier. Club skipper Duncan Forbes became his standard-bearer, synonymous with raw meat.

For Saunders, all this was a natural progression after saving Southern League Yeovil from relegation and then spelling out the working man's creed at Oxford United, where he was team boss for three months following Arthur Turner's appointment as general manager.

His admiration of Leeds – "the best thing that has happened to English football for years" – gave an early clue that Saunders was fully prepared to take the path that lacked popular appeal. Getting out of the Second Division and establishing themselves as a power in the First was often a painful process for the Yorkshire club before Don Revie milked the applause and became England manager.

◄ *"Am I pushing them too hard?" Ron Saunders welcomes back his Canaries for training on the slopes of Mousehold.*

(Picture by Alan Howard.)

I recall Saunders' antics at Orient on promotion night in April, 1972. The clenched fists, arrogant stance and emphatic "They've gotta believe us now!" He was convinced success would be achieved his way. At times, it had been an obsession. The public and Press remained sceptical for so long, it must have been an effort for Saunders to wave to the adoring hordes with true forgiveness in his heart.

The Saunders style was bound to hurt in some cases. Winger Steve Grapes once described him thus after a gruelling stint on the training beat: "He makes bloody Hitler look like Edith Cavell!" It was also claimed that Saunders made one player feel so inadequate that the poor creature dug a hole in which to hide – and then did extra training because he took too long to dig it.

Saunders certainly brought to Carrow Road a code of conduct the like of which hadn't been nailed up before, and plotted a deliberate course towards some kind of ogre-figure he considered a necessity to persuade the weak-hearted. He would not accept the "hard man" label, but he did confess to being "a bit of a swine". The distinction had to rest somewhere in that old proverb about making silk purses out of sows' ears. He produced a promotion team out of material few people considered suitable for a history-making journey.

Sweeping changes at Carrow Road didn't end at putting players through a training mangle that wrung out enough sweat to sink the River End. He dared to tamper with sacred Canary ideology on the terraces in the name of progress. "On The Ball, City!", the anthem that struck fear into opponents with such remarkable force during the 1959 Cup run, was a bit of a dirge to him.

He never heard it sweep across the ground with that kind of fervour. He insisted, however, that it represented past glories when the emphasis should have been on a promising present and a vibrant future. "Norr-idge! Norr-idge!" was approval, 1972-style.

> Ron moves in a mysterious way,
> His wonders to perform.
> Little wealth, bags of stealth,
> And a name upon the form!

I scribbled down that little verse of praise after one of Saunder's typically cool coups in the transfer market. If future generations see Mousehold as his monument, then his husbandry during a period of severe restraint must be hailed as one of the key features of his reign. (It also hastened the end of that reign.)

The path to Division One was paved with austerity signs. City were at the centre of a vicious financial circle, spotlighted by the fact that promotion year kicked off with this blunt message from the annual meeting of the shareholders: "If you want to see new faces in the side, you'll have to provide the cash." That suggestion didn't go down too well with many supporters.

The Canaries lost nearly £22,000 on the 1970–71 campaign, and that was an improvement of over £12,000 compared with the previous year. I felt at the end of Saunders' second term that his team had fallen short of requirements in an average year. They failed to string together enough entertaining performances to halt the downward trend in Carrow Road gates.

He had players on the transfer list so long it was clear any close-season deals wouldn't put much in the bank. Disturbing, for it proved that if you can't sell well, you stand no chance of buying big.

The search for another striker was a rather sad cliche. It went on throughout the summer, and when the action resumed, the situation was met with a curious mixture of sympathy and rebellion. Some suggested the launching of a "Buy A Player" Fund. Others urged a boycott of Carrow Road until that precious commodity was forthcoming. City got off to a remarkably good start.

The financial handicaps under which Saunders operated were accentuated by rigid principles from which he refused to waver. Short-term deals didn't interest him. "We are now buying to improve chances of reaching Division One." Six major signings in three years added up to justification of so-careful combing for the right material. Peter Silvester was the first to arrive for £20,000 from Reading two months after City's new boss took over. Graham Paddon (£25,000) soon followed from Coventry. Then there was a gap of 13 months before the next swoop, Doug Livermore leaving Liverpool for £22,000.

October 6th, 1971, saw the end of that frustrating hunt for a new striker. David Cross signed in for £40,000 as City scored a resounding victory over Carlisle in the League Cup. The Supporters' Club had just weighed in with a £30,000 cheque.

I have good reason to remember the other two big items on the shopping list. The Christmas Eve session for overworked but sociable journalists had reached that tantalising "it must be my round" stage, when the pub door burst open. Saunders had bought a player? Pull the other one – it's got jingle bells on! Eventually, the agitated messenger convinced us that his journey was necessary, and the news of Phil Hubbard's £20,000 move from Lincoln made the late editions of the *Eastern Evening News* amid a few murmurs about unfortunate timing and thoughtless soccer managers.

Jim Bone completed the pre-promotion buying programme. With Silvester forced out of the closing stages of the campaign by a cartilage operation, City had a new front man. The £30,000 capture from Partick Thistle filled the bill admirably. The most adventurous Canary since Hugh Curran, Bone did his best to bury City's image as an efficient but colourless force.

Saunders was in jocular mood when he unveiled his latest signing. Before the jocularity, however, came a prime example of Saunders' flair for drama – I was on the receiving end of a command performance.

It had been a hectic afternoon, with calls to Carrow Road every few minutes for a check on the latest developments. The story of the player bought to inspire the big promotion push was ready to roll, together with another

Peter Silvester, who was Ron Saunders' first signing at Carrow Road, leads the training pack as they jump to it on Mousehold.

(Picture by Alan Howard.)

"*This is hurting me just as much as it's hurting you . . .*"
(Picture by Alan Howard.)

"*There – wasn't that bad at all, was it!*"
(Picture by Alan Howard.)

tribute to the manager who defied economic restrictions. The clock had hurtled round to 3.10 when the all-clear sounded. Just in time.

Down at the ground, Saunders emerged with a deep frown and a hand held across his brow. All the cares of the soccer world were upon him. "Go and scrap the story," he muttered. "It's all off." I pointed out that I was very sorry but the edition had gone and would be adorning a few thousand teatables within the hour. The worried look gave way to a cheeky beam. He liked having the original fall-guy around the place now and again. Jim Bone stepped out of the boardroom for a chat.

Norwich City started First Division life with a 1–1 draw against Everton at Carrow Road in August, 1972. Jim Bone scored the home goal. Ron Saunders resigned as Canary manager an hour after a 3–1 Carrow Road defeat at the hands of Everton in November, 1973. All four goals were own-goals, a suitable prelude to the boardroom explosion that left struggling City without a boss. The storm clouds had been gathering for some time, and there had been stories that Saturday morning about Saunders heading for Manchester City. Let me consult my *Eastern Daily Press* notebook to provide a flavour of that eventful day:

"For once, the after-match 'inquest' deserved such a title. As if sensing a black patch in Carrow Road history, boardroom regulars went into agitated huddles. Knots of reporters paced the corridors like sentinels of doom. It was an eerie atmosphere, accentuated by Ron Saunders' appearance with a plate of cakes.

"He smiled and asked if anyone was waiting to see him, supporting claims that his men had scored all Everton's goals. 'Duncan Forbes got two and Dave Stringer the other,' he said with the dull acceptance of a man ticking off names on an extra-long Christmas shopping list. He moved on to his office – with the cakes.

"Chairman Arthur South had an equally broad smile in the boardroom as he shook hands with Everton directors and manager Billy Bingham. They said they looked forward to seeing him later in the campaign. He told us he was looking forward to reading Monday's papers, and volunteered the suggestion that the City side contained five or six players short of the necessary skills to fight Division One battles.

"As I pointed out this was evident at the end of last season, and the chairman made no attempt to disagree, a Fleet Street reporter whispered: 'Is his first name Arthur?' and made for a telephone.

"Even so, there were no strong hints of the angry confrontation to come – and the end of Ron Saunders' reign as Norwich City manager. He wrote out his resignation. The Sunday sensation stories began to roll.

"I sensed a couple of weeks ago that a top-level rift was in danger of becoming a hopeless split. When Mr South became chairman at the start of the season he said there would be 'hard words between two hard men'. Clear indications that the relationship wasn't just strained but frosting over were given when the Canaries flew to Merseyside for their League Cup-tie with Everton. The tradition of chairman and manager sitting together wasn't observed.

"Although this was one of the rare occasions when reporters travelled with the team – Saunders ended that tradition a couple of years ago – it would be naive to overlook the whispers and nods that greeted their 'separate ways' policy.

"I understand Saunders was given some kind of ultimatum about buying players shortly before collecting £150,000 for the sale of David Cross to Coventry. Undoubtedly, he had complained constantly about a shortage of ready cash, and I claimed a few weeks ago that he was likely to sell one or two of his established players before taking much-needed plunges into the transfer market.

"After that article in the *E.D.P.*, in which I suggested the club had only about £150,000 immediately available, Mr South told me at Norwich Airport, when the flight to Merseyside was held up by fog, that I had miscalculated on certain points. The real trouble, he claimed, was that the manager was not bringing possible signings to them. Money wasn't the beginning and end of their problems.

"Obviously, patience wore thin on the board as the Canaries carried an ominous struggling look this term after walking the relegation tightrope last season. Saturday's defeat by Everton stressed the extent of current anxiety. (Only ten points from 16 outings.)

"While the lack of action on the transfer front was the main bone of contention as crunch day approached, there were other contributory factors. Saunders felt on at least two occasions that the chairman had left him out in the cold.

"Mr South's 'Attacking football' pledge on succeeding Mr Geoffrey Watling as chairman wasn't greeted kindly by a manager who considered it his job to formulate any policy on the playing side.

"More recently, the Canaries found 'clean up your game' letters in their pay packets. Saunders said he knew nothing about them. The chairman, believed to have had them put there, told me it was a personal matter between the board and the players. Significantly, there was no reference to the manager.

"In whatever direction recriminations are aimed – and there's no suggestion I have painted a complete picture – it must be accepted that such a situation couldn't continue, particularly in view of City's parlous position."

John Bond became Norwich City's 11th manager since the war. Ron Saunders went to Manchester City. Shortly after his departure, with recriminations still thick in the air, the Norwich chairman took the unusual step of showing me minutes of board meetings at which the manager was strongly urged to bring possible signings to the directors.

Saunders found it hard enough to find the right sort of material to win promotion to Division One for the first time. The signings needed to stay

Duncan Forbes, Ron Saunders' standard-bearer on the pitch, shows plenty of vigour as the Canaries take off in the First Division against Everton at Carrow Road in August, 1972.

(Picture by Alan Howard.)

Jimmy Bone, who scored Norwich City's first Division One goal in the 1–1 draw with Everton. He soars to a challenge, with the late Terry Anderson looking on.

(Picture by Alan Howard.)

there? Well, perhaps that challenge was beyond both manager and directors at the time, and frustrations were bound to spill over into bitterness.

My relationship with the hard man from Birkenhead was never an easy one. I stood firm regarding the distinction between reflecting public opinion and trying to sway it. He objected to the way I approached my reporting task at times. An article criticising one of his players led to the Press being banished from the team bus, and we often went weeks without discussing club activities in any depth.

After one sharp difference of opinion on a bitterly cold morning, a shirt-sleeved manager mocked the hunched reporter, streaming with cold over the electric fire in the corner of the office. "Here you are, you snivelling wretch – a cup of tea with something in it. Probably kill you." I took it, sipped and looked him straight in the eye. "I'll be about here long after you've gone, old partner!"

He knew what I meant. He nearly smiled.

ON THE BALL, CITY!

In the days to call, which we half left behind,
Our boyhood's glorious game,
And our youthful vigour has declined
With its mirth and its lonesome end;
You will think of the time, the happy time,
Its memories fond recall
When in the bloom of the time, the happy time,
Its memories fond recall
When in the bloom of our youthful prime
We've kept upon the ball.
Kick off, throw it in, have a little scrimmage,
Keep it low, a splendid rush, bravo, win or die;
On the ball, City, never mind the danger,
Steady on, now's your chance,
Hurrah! We've scored a goal.

Let all tonight then drink with me
To the football game we love,
And wish it may successful be,
As other games of old,
And in one grand united toast
Join player, game and song
And fondly pledge your pride and toast
Success to the City club.

Kick off, throw it in, have a little
     scrimmage   etc.

Horse Power

"Horse power was much safer when the horses had it." A rich testament to a dependable feature of our agricultural past rather than just a simple indictment of a noisy, race-against-time present.

Perhaps we've added a dash or two of rural romance to the sepia pictures from yesterday's farmyards, but there can be no denying the special relationship that grew between man and horse as they struggled together in all weathers, through all seasons.

Horses were the most important creatures in East Anglia up to the last war. "Good horses, good farm" was a saying that rang true across the headlands. The men looked after the horses as well as worked with them, and took great pride in the appearance and standard of their team. There was competition among the farms – braid and ribbons, shiny coats and harness in perfect condition.

Those days on the land were long and hard, especially during the corn harvest, when teams of horses were changed halfway through the day to give them a rest. How many Norfolk lads began their working days in the fields when harvest beckoned and a "howd gee" boy was needed?

That first job in a grown-up world meant leading the horses as the harvest wagon was loaded up with corn and shouting a warning to the men on top to hold tight. In fact, the instruction seemed to vary from district to district, or at least the pronunciation did, and the debate still continues about "howd gee", "holdjer", "hold yer" and "hold ye". I plump for "howd gee" simply because it seems the most logical – "howd" for the man on the load to hold tight, and "gee" for the "hoss" to go on.

Ploughing also had a vocabulary of its own, and again it varied from one area to another: "keppier", "cubbeear", "capper", "woish" or "woosh", "cumhether" and "weasse" were all instructions from the ploughman to his horses.

Of course, they have gone with the way of life that inspired them. Each

season had its own language, and when you think of all the associated trades, like blacksmith, harness-maker and wheelwright, it becomes clear just how big a part the horse played on the Norfolk stage less than half-a-century ago.

Derek Winner, of East Dereham, provided me with this scene from a farm at Westacre, near Swaffham, in the early 1940s. A thousand acres, with over 40 horses: "Billy Bumphrey was head teamman, and his brother John one of the under-teammen. John had a very quiet voice, not much more than a whisper. He did most of the drilling with two horses, his main horse being Trimmer, a big Suffolk who would walk as straight as a die all day long, and teach the young horse alongside him. But woe betide anyone who worked John's horse, if he was on holiday, with a normal voice and shouted at the horse. You might as well pack up and go home as the horse would do nothing you wanted for the rest of the day." A perfect example of his master's voice!

"Wilson", of West Tofts, near Mundford, has a fund of horse stories, many of them the legacy of her days in the land army. "There were eight working horses on the farm. The horseman's name was Alec and he was rather a moody man. Although I was shown how to drive a tractor, I was sometimes sent to help Alec for a few days at a time. I soon noticed that Alec sucked his bad teeth, making a sort of squeaking noise when he was near the horses or if he was in a bad mood.

"Early in the mornings Alec fetched the horses into the stable from the yard or field about an hour before the rest of the farm men arrived. The horses were given a feed of crushed oats and chaff and brushed down ready for work. I was told to watch out for the horse called Captain because he had rather a spiteful temper.

"One morning, Alec was delayed. After waiting for a time, I decided to have a go at getting the horses in on my own. I put the feed in the wooden manger. Each horse had its own place and knew where to stand. The horses looked powerful and massive, and after speaking to each by name I boldly walked up and fastened the chain around each horse's neck. After struggling to carry a bag of crushed oats from the barn I started to refill the stable's corn bin.

"Suddenly, I heard the sound of heavy hooves on the cobbled stable floor. I looked round and to my horror I saw that the unfastened chain had slipped from Captain's neck and he was loose in the stable. I shouted – but this seemed to annoy him. The huge horse put back his ears and came clumping down the stable towards me. I threw the remains of the bag of oats into the bin and banged the lid shut. As the horse got nearer I ran and jumped into the chaff box, pulling the lid down behind me. The dreaded horse stood a foot or two away, breathing and snorting.

"After what seemed ages I heard Alec standing his bike against the outer wall. As he entered the stable, he shouted: 'Hey up! What's gorn on in here?'

◀ *Land Army girls helping with the harvest at Besthorpe, near Attleborough, during the last war.*

(Picture provided by George Marsh, of Brandiston.)

Suffolk Punches ready for a long stint with a double plough.

Three's company along the furrows.

All hands to the harvest — and the youngsters can join in.

Alec laughed like anything when he saw my frightened eyes and serious face looking out from under the lid."

"Wilson" also recalls visits by the stallion man to the farms where they took considerable pride in breeding good horses for the heavy work on the land. "The stallions were paraded on market day during spring. Each farmer took his pick and booked the number of mares to be covered. A week or two later, the man and his stallion visited each district.

"Sometimes the stallion man travelled in a dealer's cart drawn by a pony, with the stallion tied to the back of the cart. The dealer's cart contained a bale or two of hay and food for the horses. It was often usual for the man, the pony and the stallion to stay at a farm overnight. The whole village stopped work briefly when the stallion passed by. If the children were not at school, the farmer's wife hastily dispatched them to visit their Granny or Aunt in the village, telling them to remain there until they were collected. This avoided too many embarrassing questions!"

The transition from horses to machinery wasn't without its traumas. Herbert, the horseman of long-standing, was being instructed in the art of using the blue Fordson Major tractor and the powerlift furrow plough. He stalled the engine in the middle of the field. Herbert dismounted and gave a quick pull on the starting handle. The tractor was still hot and still in gear. It started up at once and began to buck in an alarming fashion. Herbert jumped back, waved his cap and kept on shouting: "Whoa, yer bugger! Whoa yer bugger – Whoa!"

That special relationship between man and horse has been given a permanent setting in John Kett's delightful Norfolk dialect poem, "Harry The Hossman". For those not too familiar with the local vernacular, let me point out that "harpin tuds" are "hopping toads" and "pishmires" are ants. Between them, old Harry and John Kett have drawn a Norfolk picture where people are still in close touch with nature, and still finding respect for traditions:

One man with two horses ... harrowing near Acle.
(Picture by Clifford Temple.)

HARRY THE HOSSMAN

Ole Harry were a Norfolk man,
Ah, that he were, right t'rew;
He wholly loved the countraside,
An' spuk the language, tew.
He knew most evra fild around,
The hedges, woods, an all;
A rea' strong feller he were, tew,
Though he weren't all that tall.
He'd hump up on his shou'ders loods
No other man couln't carra –
Why, bor, he'd hev'em shifted
While they went to find a barrer!

. . . He'd bin a so'ger long ago,
Then come back on the land.
An' how he loved his hosses!
He jus' couln't understand
How they could dew wi'out 'em
When tractors come along,
Fer a faarm wi'out no hosses
Fared to him a faarm gone wrong.

Well, one day we stood maardlin',
An' I say to him, I say,
"I hear yew'a bin a maaster one
Wi' hosses, in yar day."
He stared at me right haard like,
An' give a rea' owd look;
"Tha's trew," hc says, "an' I tell yew
That din't come from no book!
If yew'd be good wi' hosses
Yew on'y want one thing –
Tha's one o' them there harpin tuds
What come around in spring,
An' then yew find a pishmires' nest,
An' stick that tud right in it,
An' laater on yew taake it out –
Yew oon't ha' need t'skin it!"

I reckon when he got that far
I must ha' kind o' smiled;
He say, "Yew're thinkin' tha's a lie!"
I thought he might git wild!
"Why no," I say. "Dew yew go on
An' tell yer story, dew!"
"Oright," he say, "as long as yew
Remember tha's all trew . . .
Now, them there little bones yew'a got,
Wi'out no flesh na skin,
Yew taake'em tew a runnin' stream,
An' yew just hull'em in."
"Why, then yew'll luse'em all," I say.
Ole Harry whispered low,
"Tha's where yew're wrong – they'll floot, they
    will;
Ah, that sound straange, I know.
Them bones'll go a-floatin' down,
But there'll be one what oon't,
An' that'll go the other way –
Yew jus' see if that don't!"

"Now hold yew on," I say, "that seem
A rum ole dew t'me."
"Well, that int all," ole Harry say,
"Now listen here. Y'see
That bone what go orf UP the stream,
Yew keep it; from that day
Wi' evra hoss yew come acrorst
Yew'll allus hev yar way."

Tha's what he telled me, an' y'know
He meant it, evra waad,
An' I think on it evra time
I see a harpin' tud.
Now, if yew don't believe this taale
I s'pus I'll understand,
But dew yew know, wi' enna hoss
He were a rea' dab hand!
An' one thing more jus' come t'me
Wha's warth a-thinkin' on –
They'll likelier hev hosses there,
Than tractors, where he's gone;
An' if tha's so, well, likely tew
There's harpin tuds there, bor –
An' he'll look arter hosses
Like he done so well afore!

That's the drill with horses to the fore at Hockering.
(Picture by Clifford Temple.)

Hemsby ploughman Sidney Knights and his helpers.

Golden Smiles

PICTURES BY LES GOULD

Young Albert was afforded the lion's share of publicity when he went to Blackpool and got a bit more than fresh air and fun. Of course, if you swallow that little tale you'll help keep the true spirit of music hall alive.

Seaside entertainment, thankfully, can still find room for the odd slice of outrageous nostalgia along with all the trappings of the video era. Why, our coastline publicity moguls have been known to use "The Good Old Days" as an inducement rather than just as an apology on behalf of those who like to dip into the past.

Remember how your sense of childhood wonder was sharpened by seaside sights and sounds? You didn't have to be a Young Albert anxious to do mischief, poking out a stick with a horse's head handle: bucket and spade and five bob for the funfair would do.

Perhaps familiarity and availability feed cynicism a bit earlier these days. Blame motor cars and television if you like. But there must still be a few thousand tingles to spare when the family on holiday, or just paying a visit, size up the live shows on offer.

There is no adequate substitute – and I've checked with the performers as well. Comedians, singers, musicians, ventriloquists, jugglers, actors, summer-seasoned campaigners, young hopefuls at the bottom of the bill . . . a big majority say it's the only way to find and keep the real rapport between artist and audience.

While I was on local newspaper duty at Great Yarmouth in the mid-1960s, I relished the chance to chat with several stars who had come to terms with a new era. They'd honed their trades in the music halls, and were now earning big money in the television studios.

One of my idols, Jimmy Wheeler, confided one night at the Windmill that

"With his little box of bloaters in his hand ..." George Formby and wife Beryl at Yarmouth in 1949.

"Zip Goes A Pillion!" George wishes 'em luck in the Great Yarmouth T.T. Races.

"I've arrived – and to prove it I'm here!" Max Bygraves touches down for laughter and song at the Britannia Pier in 1950.

"Lovely wedding – even the cake is in tiers!" Max attends a happy event in between houses on the pier.

"I'll sing the Adoration Waltz while I'm here!" David Whitfield signs up for the season.

"The Finger of Suspicion Points at You!" Dickie Valentine has the law on his side as the fans crush forward in 1955.

Double act looking for chain reaction ... mirth pedallers Nat Jackley and Stan Stennett on the 1957 Tour De Golden Mile.

"And here is my impression of Lester Piggott taking off for Royal Ascot ..." Peter Goodwright ready for the Laughter Stakes on Donkey Oatie.

"Hallo my darlings!" Charlie Drake is the one in the middle looking for Eastern promise in 1960.

Talent on tap beside the sea as a dozen Tiller Girls step out for the 1958 routine.

"Come into my parlour ..." Yarmouth Mayor John Winter (left) entertains The Beverley Sisters, along with former England football captain Billy Wright in 1963.

Coach and pair – singers Pearl Carr and Teddy Johnson take the air, while Vic Oliver takes the reins in 1958.

Hugh and cry in 1966. Terry Scott and Hugh Lloyd open the Yarmouth Pleasure Beach for the summer season.

Bob's Full House – 1961-style. Autograph hunters keep Master Monkhouse at full stretch.

Who's that under the hat?

You lucky people! It's Tommy Trinder.

A comic cut of the cards – just like that! Tommy Cooper working on his act in 1958.

"Nice of you to speak to Francis!" Busy times for Frankie Howerd in 1961.

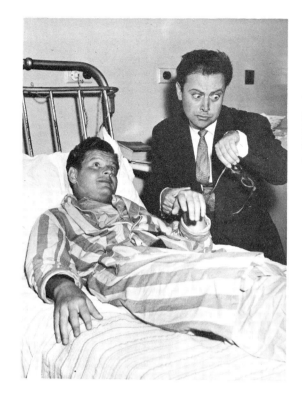

"Blimey! Time for me to take over." Doctor Derek Roy down Bedpan Alley with Benny Hill in 1957. Derek replaced Benny in the summer show after he'd been taken ill with appendicitis.

They raised much more than half a sixpence! Charity football at The Wellesley in 1961 with a showbiz flavour. Tommy Steele shakes hands with Emile Ford before the kick-off.

Dickie Henderson about to lead the umpire a real song and dance in the stars' cricket match of 1966. ▶

"It could be quite chilly by the time I ◀ *reach my century ..." Al Read on his way to the crease in 1957.*

Will the umpire strike back? Terry Scott has the batsman in his sights in 1966. ▶

Where's the ball? Jimmy Tarbuck sizes up the net result (1965).

Ready, Neddy, Goon! Harry Secombe shows weighty form (1962).

Innings with no strings attached for singer Karl Denver (1966).

Jimmy and Ben top the bill in 1956.

Eric and Ern prove a bumper attraction.

Jewel and Warriss – with Patti Lewis the gem in the middle.

Lenny the Lion shares a tale with Terry Hall.

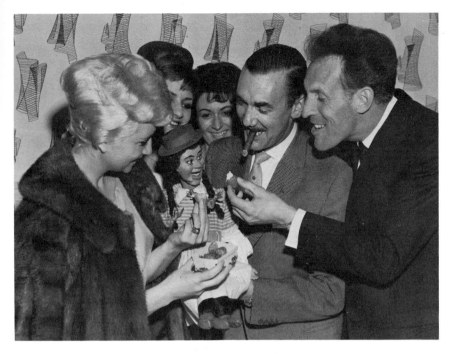

Bruce Forsyth tries to woo Daisy Mae with strawberries and cream in 1962. He's been dispensing plenty of fruit ever since.

BELOW: Galaxy of stars from 1955 – The Beverley Sisters, Tommy Trinder, Charlie Chester, Billy Whittaker and Ronnie Ronalde.

*No strangers on the shore
... and a spot of nautical advice for
Marty Wilde, Billy Fury and Karl
Denver in 1962.*

*We're no mugs! Des O'Con-
nor and Jimmy Tarbuck celebrate
Donkey Derby delight in 1968.*

real entertainment belonged on a stage with an audience out front. As he pushed back the famous battered trilby and tuned his violin, he chuckled: "They might not tell you, but a lot of them round here do summer seasons to keep sane!"

He wouldn't elaborate – "Ay-ay, thass yer lot!" – but I picked up several other hints about the seaside being good for your sanity as I haunted dressing-rooms two decades ago. Frankie Howerd, Dick Emery, Arthur Askey, Mike and Bernie Winters, Morecambe and Wise, Peter Goodwright, Rolf Harris, Tommy Cooper, Des O'Connor, Jimmy Clitheroe ... such a list of laughter-raisers, and how often they'd raise a hand to make you listen as the roars went up for someone else on the bill. Peter Goodwright also showed a compassion-ate streak – he gave me decent marks for my impression of Captain Pugwash. (Seven out of ten.)

Perhaps many of the singers knew they were shining in a more ephemeral world, with pop tastes changing at an alarming rate. But it's with genuine affection that I recall names like Duffy Power, Johnny Gentle, Vince Eager and Karl Denver. Then there was Dickie Pride – and you have to admit that sounds a deal more friendly than Sid Vicious or Johnny Rotten!

Be fair, some warblers had more durable qualities. Billy Fury, Marty Wilde, Frank Ifield, Lonnie Donnegan, Donald Peers. Ah, Donald Peers, who was once advised to write his autobiography if only to urge people to "Buy a Babbling Book". I once caught him on the raw by asking how it felt making a comeback. "My dear boy," he sighed "... I've never been away."

It all depends how old you are as to where you pitch your version of "The Good Old Days". In offering mine, I have to strike one or two notes of regret. I never saw George Formby or Max Miller on stage, and a national newspaper never did pay up for some telling quotes I phoned over on the night it was announced Jimmy Tarbuck was taking over as compere of "Sunday Night at the London Palladium". It took me four hours of hanging around the Welling-ton Pier stage door to get them. Perhaps I should have stuck a "Press" ticket in my hat like they used to in the old films.

On the credit side, I give heartfelt thanks that I had a cup of tea with Eric Morecambe and watched Tommy Cooper sort out some of his props. To this day I can't understand why he didn't hit me when I said I couldn't remember his name – but the fez was familiar.

A risky business, sowing seeds along the Golden Mile just to brighten up your memories. But more rewarding in the long run than mucking about with lions pretending to be friendly.

Buttercup Time

PICTURES BY JOHN MARR

" A rural cricket match in buttercup time, seen and heard through the trees; it is surely the loveliest scene in England and the most disarming sound. From the ranks of the unseen dead for ever passing along our country lanes on their eternal journey, the Englishmen fall out for a moment to look over the gate of the cricket field and smile."

– Sir James Barrie.

I can't imagine life without cricket, simply because it's been with me from the start. Crackling commentaries on the old wireless, with father demanding hush at the teatable as the 1948 Australians took away some of the taste. How we loathed Bradman for putting Dad in a bad mood just as another innings beckoned from the orchard! "But it's my turn to be Hutton. . . ." In fact, it was my turn to be washed and put to bed.

The release from Chapel on a Sunday afternoon, and subsequent charge towards the village pitch near the war memorial. Beeston *versus* Longham – just as important as any Test match, and worthy of my budding John Arlott impression as I pedalled furiously to the scene of rural combat.

Those games often brought entire families out to play. Uncles and older brothers in the team. Father umpiring. Mother and sisters doing the teas. I made my mark as the village scorer, and that must have been prophetic. The pen has always been mightier than the willow in my hand.

There was always the chance that someone's bike would break down, or a cow would start calving at an awkward time. "Put the boy down at number eleven." Excitement and dread make a potent cocktail as the ball hurtles towards you through the nettles and thistles, and the rest of the side urge you to get it in. It disappears through the barbed wire. You swear back so quietly they can't hear you.

I recall our village team meeting at the post office, already changed into whites, if they had them, waiting for Ralph Cross to arrive with the official

Don Rayner, who brought a smile to Horsford club cricket for many years.

Eric Bedwell – his organising flair helped fashion the success of the Bob Carter Cup competition, started in 1969.

We have lift-off! George Slater of Beccles falls to a spectacular catch by the Norwich Union wicket-keeper.

Dereham stalwart Ian Battelley at the crease. He and his brothers have contributed so much to local sport in recent years.

team coach – his lorry. We all piled into the back and headed for the wilds of Gateley, Rougham, Tittleshall. . . .

I often had the lorry to myself as darkness fell after the game. I could hear them singing and laughing in the pub. My rations of Vimto and crisps had long since vanished.

Dereham cricket ground was the setting for the Mid-Norfolk Shield Final on August Bank Holiday Monday, and it didn't matter very much that your lot hadn't got there. It was the villagers' day out, ranking alongside the annual trip to the seaside as a summer ritual for sharing. The big tent where old men's memories mingled with tobacco smoke, and the youngsters clutched bottles and straws outside. Cheers of delight from the Foulsham supporters as the catch was taken inches inside the boundary.

Groans of dismay from the Rougham followers, shuffling with discomfort every time they peered towards the scoreboard. Over the years, they all had their fair share of misery and mirth. I was impartial. Just there for the occasion.

I didn't see a rural uprising to match it until Swardeston hit the Haig Village Cup trail in the 1970s. That memorable run in a national competition helped put Swardeston into the senior club ranks in Norfolk, and the players and officials know how much they owe to the villagers who trekked to all parts of the country to support them. It all came to life at Audley End in Essex on a sunswept Sunday afternoon. The lovely country house provided the perfect backcloth for the Swardeston faithful strung out along the river bank like Red Indians who'd found a new reservation. For several weekends after that, Swardeston was a ghost village as the cricketers played Pied Piper to an old-fashioned community spirit we feared had been bowled out.

The game has changed considerably since my early days as a statistician, when it was still doubtful practice to play someone in the side who didn't live or work in the village. Local team meant just that. Perhaps the competitive edge has been sharpened even more by the formation and rapid expansion of leagues and the introduction of new cup contests. Many of us mourn the passing of the good old friendly, not least because the average performer could be given a run in those fixtures where results weren't all-important.

Nowadays, points are often preferred to pints, and that also puts extra pressure on umpires. Surely that is one of the main reasons why the majority of the older players are reluctant to stay with the game and pull on the white coat.

I've collected far more stories than runs or wickets in twenty odd years with Caister-On-Sea C.C., and also found time to jot down a list of my favourite village grounds. Merton Hall, the family seat of Lord Walsingham, Old Buckenham and Brisley Green come out on top.

One of my favourite little yarns from the early 1950s concerns the Frettenham player who found it warm going at Wood Norton. One delivery came a bit high, and Bob let it hit his thigh. He felt a sharp, stinging pain and slapped

Evergreen Eddie Symonds behind the stumps for Rackheath. He celebrated his 79th birthday during the 1986 season – and that was his 65th successive season with the club!

Confident appeals from the Mallards' keeper and close fielders – and an Acle batsman is on his way back to the pavilion.

No doubt about this dismissal on the old wicket at Horsford.

Bike on the boundary for a quick getaway?

the spot. A big cloud of white smoke billowed out. He'd left his matches in his pocket, and the box was completely burnt out! As he went off for treatment, it is rumoured he was greeted by an impromptu chorus of "Singe Something Simple...."

So you think you know your cricket ... What have Old Trafford, 1887, and Shropham, 1982, got in common? Please press your buzzers. Both grounds saw play held up by swarms of bees. A century ago, so many bees flew on to the ground during the Lancashire–Surrey match, players were forced to take shelter in the pavilion. The more recent epic between Shropham and Hales was also bedevilled by bees, and play was held up five minutes either side of the tea interval.

Any cricket bag of memories must include a big pile of newspaper cuttings, recalling outstanding matches and characters who fashioned them. If I'm pushed to select just two little chapters from Norfolk's sporting past at buttercup time, I go for the very first article I wrote for the *Eastern Daily Press* sports page – and a yellowed column from the *Norwich Mercury* of 1906.

I went to see Arthur Cason at the end of the 1963 cricket season. He was 85, and the last of the underarm bowlers of Norfolk.

He played for Mileham, starting as a lad of 16 in the mid 1890s. Mileham were the top-dogs in those days, winning the Mid-Norfolk Shield four years running just before the end of the century.

"I remember the old village parson doing his bit to keep us boys keen by coming up to the practice ground and offering sixpence to anyone who could knock a single wicket back." A few more puffs on his pipe, and Arthur had left his Dereham home for the Bank Holiday atmosphere of Lexham Park in the early years of the century. "We always went there for our annual August Monday match and had a right good time with slap-up meals and all the trimmings. When old Major Keppel died his son moved to Norwich, but, do you know, he still came down to play with us, arriving in his horse and buggy – a real gentleman he was."

All social barriers were flattened for a time on the cricket field there was Arthur the yardman bowling to the Major's son. But there were still some players who thought they were entitled to certain privileges not mentioned in the rule-book.

"We were playing at Weasenham Park one afternoon when they had a county wicket-keeper behind the stumps. He was really good, but he thought he could take the ball in front of the wicket. Nothing was said until I went into bat. I had a quiet word with him, explaining that he just couldn't do that. He was right nasty, so I complained to the umpire, schoolmaster Wigg."

Evidently, the wicket-keeper's reputation outweighed schoolmaster Wigg's ideas of fair play. The only comment he made was a nervous "Be quiet Arthur, be quiet!" to the injured party. But if anything just wasn't cricket on the field of play, Arthur was not afraid to point it out.

Well, it was negligence on the part of an umpire that robbed him of two

John Edrich shows his power as the crowds flock to Ingham.

Bill Edrich in his club days with Ingham faces John Tythcott.

victims that would have taken one Saturday afternoon tally to nine. He was bowling on Hempton Green in a strong wind when the ball appeared to him to go straight through the stumps twice without disturbing the bails. No-one believed Arthur – but he took the ball and proved it. He had to be satisfied with what was then a career best of 7 for 19.

"I used to put an extra hour in every night on the farm during the cricket season so I could get away on a Saturday afternoon. It was nothing for me to walk to Wendling and back for a game of cricket."

Arthur Cason – the scourge of Mid-Norfolk batsmen nearly a century ago.

The 1906 cutting from the *Norwich Mercury* carries much more than a report of the Norfolk Club and Ground *v* Mid-Norfolk Village Shield cricket match played at Lexham Park. It acts as the perfect memento of the woman who sent it to me – Ethel Battelley, mother of those talented lads who have lit up so many Norfolk cricket grounds.

She cleared up behind me and the other reporters at the *Dereham and Fakenham Times* office in the early 1960s, and we had several little reunions before she died. Our last meeting was on Dereham Cricket Ground when Caister reached the Norfolk Junior Cup semi-finals in the summer of 1983. It was my first playing appearance on a ground where I'd watched and reported countless games. Dereham A gave us a good hiding. Ethel and I had a good mardle.

She found the newspaper cutting in the lining of an old trunk – and immediately thought of me. (The old, brown and withered connection, I suppose.) An unexpected harvest for the bowlers is the main topic of the match report. The Shield representative side had to do without F. Bales, the Billingford bowler who met with so much success in the corresponding match of 1905. Slipping on a rail at Wymondham Station, Bales fell and broke a bone in his left wrist.

Club and Ground won by 65 runs. In fact, the Shield eleven went in for a second time, but when they'd reached 14 for the loss of Pope's wicket, a heavy thunderstorm put paid to play for the day. I reproduce the two innings that counted as a small tribute to the Norfolk villages where cricket has flourished over the decades. They didn't beat the county club side on this occasion – but it might have been different if F. Bales hadn't slipped at the railway station.

MID-NORFOLK VILLAGE SHIELD

E. Pope (Fakenham) b Smith 12
J. Burton (Lyng) b Smith 4
E. Peachment (Billingford) b Gibson 5
Rev. L. C. Streatfield (Weasenham) b Smith 0
E. M. Webb (Swanton) c Gascoigne b Gibson 4
A. Mayes (Billingford) b Smith 0
B. Bagnall (Hoe) b Smith 0
E. Wier (Elsing) c Prior b Gibson 11
R. Makins (Litcham) not out 10
W. Ridley (Litcham) c Smith b Gibson 0
J. Meachen (Elmham) c Gascoigne b Gibson 0
F. Osbiston (Lexham) c Gibson b Smith 5
Extra 1
Total 52

CLUB AND GROUND

E. E. Darly b Ridley 0
G. A. Stevens b Ridley 6
F. W. Swann c and b Ridley 1
E. Chapman b Ridley 9
Capt. Gascoigne c and b Bagnall 12
B. W. A. Keppel b Ridley 21
C. T. Gowing b Bagnall 0
E. G. Burton c and b Peachment 5
C. B. L. Prior b Peachment 6
S. D. Page not out 31
Gibson c Pope b Peachment 0
Smith c Burton b Wier 21
Extras 5
Total 117

Fair Comment

The following are excerpts from articles first published in the *Norfolk Fair* magazine under the heading of "Fair Comment". As many of them carry a topical flavour, I give the dates of their appearance.

JUNE, 1984

Norfolk's nostalgia buffs are having a field day. As the battle between conservation and commercialism continues to demand more honesty than most of the combatants can offer, there's a strong temptation to dive into the hedgerows of the past. Should be safe in there...

Watch the horses and binders chew up and spit out the harvest under cloudless August skies. Savour the throb of the threshing ritual, with clouds of dust ascending and dogs ready for the rats below. Listen to the Christmas carols bouncing off the ceiling of the old village chapel.

Enjoy a day out at the seaside, donkeys and doughnuts vying for your pennies. Dance in the school playground if it's not your turn to wind up the gramophone. Hop on a steam train into yesterday's tunnels.

Ignore the cynics who ask, ever so politely, how on earth you're managing to survive without rickets, ringworm and rationing.

That's the real trouble. The middle ground is being shunned. Those who cherish the past are too scared of the future to make much sense of the present. Those who scoff at all our yesterdays are too anxious to get today out of the way as well. Dragging feet versus mechanised mayhem?

I don't live in an old hedgerow, but I'm fond of my memories of Norfolk village life when it took individuality as the key to collective pride during the years after the last war. From thatcher to shepherd, lay preacher to fastest bowler in the local cricket team, and chapel organist to the best pub singer, they all did it for their own satisfaction which was heightened and sweetened by gratitude and praise from their neighbours.

That's the kind of achievement worth preserving – or reviving if it has disappeared. New housing estates and dormitory villages can squeeze that spirit dry, so it's mainly up to those who know its true worth to them to turn the signpost towards the past and take the "old-fashioned" jeers in their stride.

JULY, 1984

There's another record entry for Norfolk's Best-Kept Village Competition. No doubt, this contest inspires a brand of community spirit and effort well worth keeping alive – even if comparisons must be odious to those who have to surrender so much terrain to holiday caravans and chalets along our coastline.

I've been on a spying mission into the heart of title-seeking territory. Several villages, and a few towns, take pride all the year round in their reputations for neatness and tidiness. They're bound to have their shoes polished to mount the podium for the August accolades. For the majority, however, it's a case of looking for some decent footwear. Finding the laces to match for the big inspection simply reminds them of stern schoolteachers and barking sergeant-majors who relished flaws in the parade.

Perhaps it all boils down to the fact that some communities – like some families – are naturally more tidy than others. Bringing errant characters into line can be a tricky job. For instance, what can you do with a rustic dreamer who laps up Mary Russell Mitford's "Our Village" and its evocative sketches of life in the early 19th century?

You get the picture.... "the road was a playground – ducks, chickens, pigs and children scattered over all." Not to mention the poachers, gipsies and vagabonds abounding in the hemlock, doing their best to avoid the stocks in the village or the treadmill in the next town.

Now ask your rustic dreamer to put scissors and hoover to work around the village green, and attach a bucket and spade to every dog going about its daily business. You'll get a tidy answer, and a few suggestions as to where you might like to stick the list of volunteers on border duty.

As the appeal to parochial pride nips round nostalgia corner and heads for more fertile plains, the romantics have to make way for the realists. They have some sympathy with the brush-and-dustpan brigade, but warn strongly against cutting down all vegetation and mowing all the verges in the name of tidiness.

Nature isn't tidy, and precious flora and fauna can be obliterated in the annual pursuit of points. Refuges are vital to the world of wildlife we've taken for granted since that impromptu adventure among the brambles on the long way back from Sunday School. Really, it's surprising that the spirit of conservation is so strong among those with painful memories of torn trousers and

◀ *"Wonder who lives in this little harvest house ..."*

(Picture by Clifford Temple.)

Horses and hands to the fore in this Norfolk harvest scene from 1911.
(Picture provided by Victor Dewing, of Briston.)

scratched legs – especially when a clip round the ear was the automatic follow-up on arriving home!

There have been calls from some who've recovered that our Best-Kept Village Competition should be just as much about good nature management as pruning and preening in readiness for the judges. Difficult to assess, maybe, but there's no doubt that such pleas are rooted in care for tomorrow as well as delight in yesterday.

How many village ponds have been filled in since you were young? Many were a natural centre-piece, a rich adventure playground for young and old alike. Rusty bikes and bedsteads may have made life hard for the water-hens and frogs – but were they all beyond redemption? Ponder on....

How many healthy trees have come under the axe in your neck of the woods in the past decade? What about the number of amputated hedgerows along the lanes where you biked or strolled to fill your jar with blackberries?

It's up to you to decide if our rural housekeeping is up to scratch in Norfolk. But as that well-swept podium beckons, let's look for a balance between picture-postcard perfection and the natural world we're asked to share.

☆   ☆   ☆   ☆

I spend most of my days off renewing acquaintance with bits of Norfolk that hold special memories – but there are little voyages of discovery as well. One of the most recent took in a shoal of parishes in the Fakenham–Wells–Hunstanton triangle.

It was with a tinge of guilt that I nodded for the first time towards Waterden, Bagthorpe, Choseley and Tattersett. And many others seemed to ask where I'd been for so many years.

The only reasonable answer is that Norfolk is a big county, and it's impossible to keep in regular touch with all corners, even in these days of speed and mobility. The coast claims our interest at all times of the year, but there are scores of villages that hardly ever see a stranger or an old friend.

Sport does build many local bridges, with cricketers, footballers, bowls and darts players piling into other neighbourhoods, often for the first time as the result of promotion or relegation. Out comes the road map for hazardous trips into the unknown. The journey home finds time for voting ... smashing little ground, their green has a slope at the bottom, the board wasn't straight but the barmaid's better than ours.

That's only one area where new links are forged. Women's Institutes and other travel-hungry organisations do their bit. But it seems strange to assume that more people in Swaffham have been to Ibiza or Malta than Irstead or Mautby. Even stranger to suggest the majority would find it hard to pinpoint those Norfolk villages.

In the fond hope that a Norfolk twinning programme can develop naturally in the next few years, I'll point the way. Irstead is three miles south of Stalham; Mautby is five miles north-west of Great Yarmouth.

Now, good people of Dersingham have a day out at Wickhampton.

AUGUST, 1984

I'm lapping up a good summer on the fete circuit. Not that you're likely to get too big-headed on being elevated to the "personality" peerage in Norfolk.

"We usually get someone famous to open our event, but we thought we'd have a change this year," they say with the sort of wink that makes you wonder if the committee are doing it for a dare.

Popping out of the wireless set on to the village green can cause confusion as well. There's the little old lady passing by. She stops to tell you that you sound taller on the radio. And her sister wants a copy of that recipe for Norfolk dumplings the woman from Mulbarton sent in three years ago.

The weather provides more obvious hazards. Earlier this summer I went to Thornham, near Hunstanton, with the aim of opening the village playing field before all the fun of the fete was unfurled. It didn't stop to rain, and the stalls and sideshows were transferred to the local drill hall.

Even so, the true spirit of the eagerly-awaited day was not lost. A puckish committee member came up trumps with the ace of spades. He dug up a chunk of dripping turf to place with due solemnity on the hall stage – a symbol of rural defiance as I urged them to make use of their splendid outside facilities when the elements allowed.

Fetes of all shapes and sizes dominate the country scene as soon as the organisers think it might be safe to take a gamble on the climate. The search for fresh attractions to lure customers and boost takings looks after the rest of the year. Majorettes, jazz buskers, pipe bands, aerobic formation teams, yard-of-ale drinkers, swings and roundabouts ... they all line up with the traditional tombola stall and the smiling duo introducing the "guess the weight of the cake" competition as if they've just invented it.

The annual spectacular at the Cheshire Home at East Carleton, near Norwich, brought the chance to drive away in a brand new car, glinting in the sun. All you had to do was throw a full house of seven sixes on a roll of the giant dice. They'd taken out insurance against such a turn-up. The car wasn't won.

In the tiny village of Ovington, near Watton, six Victorian pennies formed the most teasing test of the afternoon. They'd come to light when volunteers were working in the village hall, preparing the way for a new floor. The coins were cleaned, mounted and framed. All you had to do was guess the date on each one to win a prize. Plenty of scope on the entry card – 1837 to 1901. That much information was free.

There'll be more novel twists along the fund-raising trail next summer, with the pennies turning into thousands of pounds for the hall, church,

pavilion, school or anything else that needs constant community backing. If you have a bright idea, I'm sure your local organisers will be delighted to put it on the list. A skateboard race for the pensioners could be a winner. I'm a bit surprised something to do with ferrets hasn't caught on.

Pillow fights on the greasy pole may be due for a revival. Hurling dumplings is a bit messy, and potentially lethal if they're still in the saucepan.

If you want to play safe, just look for the ladies with the cake. Ask if they're going metric.

SEPTEMBER, 1984

As soon as the art of name-dropping meant a place in grown-up conversations, I told anyone who'd listen that a very famous sportsman was born in my home village of Beeston, near Dereham.

They'd go down the usual tracks to soccer, cricket, horse-racing, tennis ... or was it that chap who killed 157 twice in the same match on the Ploughshare darts board? You could tell they were losing interest. Time to land the knockout blow.

"Only Jem Mace – you know, the father of modern scientific boxing!" If they simply shrugged, or didn't seem too impressed, I'd reel off all the facts and figures culled from a book where I'd discovered my first hero. Unabashed by adult apathy, I continued to spread the Mace gospel. Only a few years ago, Beeston's most famous son was properly honoured by the unveiling of a memorial in the village.

Now I can knuckle down to the point. Local rivalry. You see, we young Beeston Braves, fed on Mace's mighty exploits, stole into the parish next door to give them Litcham Louts a few good swigs of pugilistic medicine. They hadn't got a cricket team. So they had to be cissies. We had Jem Mace on our side. We knew the ropes when it came to a good old bundle.

Our September sortie would allow us to march away victorious under the cloak of darkness. Litcham Common was the appointed battlefield. The verbal sparring echoed across the gorse, bramble and heath. Impromptu scuffles sent the birds scurrying. The first official bout ended in blood and tears, both of them mine, as Billy Askew caught me flush on the nose with his opening punch.

Few of my colleagues fared any better, and we had to settle for an ignominious retreat, pedalling furiously as shame chased us all the way home.

That was the last showdown. Future visits to the Common were confined to shouting and chasing along the touchline at football matches, with bigger Beeston boys close at hand, on and off the pitch, to make sure rustic hostilities didn't break out again. The Litcham Lot could hit harder. We'd found that out.

◄ *Majestic partnership from the past. Harvesting near Holt.*

(Picture by Clifford Temple.)

But they still had to envy our association with Jem Mace. What comparable names could they drop in the school playground?

I'm still proud of the Mace connections, and many other Norfolk villages can point to famous characters who have coloured their little slice of history. Litcham, meanwhile, has put up a bold signpost to the future – on that same Common where unsophisticated rivalry came to a bloody head back in the 1950s.

The first local nature reserve to be set up in the county for 17 years has been officially opened on Litcham Common. We were too busy to notice the natural riches spread out before us that September evening. I saw stars rather than oak and birch woodland. Billy Askew didn't seem obsessed with flora and fauna. Now, honour is satisfied. Beeston's got Jem Mace. Litcham's got a gem – and plenty in reserve.

OCTOBER, 1984

One of the posher Sunday papers gave us this little gem a few weeks ago: "The contemporary English village is as much the nodal point of change, flux, tension and collision as the big city from which it is popularly supposed to be a portmanteau refuge." Discuss in not less than two pints.

Of course, there are many misconceptions about village life. One old boy with a loving feel for long words he pretended not to understand once told me I was one of them. I'd mucked up a simple job on the farm, so his amiable chastisement was fully deserved, although it wasn't until I got home and thought about it that the full glory of his rustic wit seeped through.

This was the same old boy who teased his colleagues with a home-made quiz as they took a break in the harvest field. "Here's a good-un – how dew yew fynd a womun owt?" No replies, but he'd wait a full minute before providing the answer. "Wuh, thass eezy entit ... yew go rownd when she ent at hoom!" Crusts and half-eaten apples rained all over his smirking face.

When I tell these little stories to my city friends, I do play fair. He was an exception to the rural rule. It wasn't all bonhomie and dazzling banter. Most days in the field were mundane, although the fresh air gave us an appetite that compensated for the lack of a Chinese takeaway behind the freshly-built stack.

It's more fun to romanticise, and the English village in all its traditional splendour has been given the full treatment by people with more altruistic motives than estate agents. Roses round the cottage door ... donkeys munching on the village green ... youngsters leap-frogging across the school playground ... pensioners mardling outside the pub ... a chat about the weather and Mrs Formby's lumbago at the local shop ... collecting jumble for chapel roof funds ... waiting for the bus into town to order the wedding outfit.

Of such stuff are immigrants' dreams made! They'll have no truck with that squalid quarter of change, flux, tension and collision. This is Norfolk, and the dreams have been known to last for more than a fortnight.

I found a born-again realist prepared to put the whole matter in perspective with a letter to one of the posher Sunday papers. It seemed too intrusive to ask which village he had sampled, but he assured me other would-be settlers would be writing soon. Here's an extract to make all Norfolk natives think....

"And how are you supposed to forge links of friendship with people you simply cannot understand? They refuse to dress for dinner, and prefer mild beer to full-bodied wine. The local hostelry closed within a week of my arrival and there's not a decent nightclub for miles.

"I went to one function at the village hall, just to be sociable, and was obliged to buy raffle tickets between the waltz and the foxtrot. But my main complaint must be directed towards the local authority who, in their infinite wisdom, have refused me permission to build a very attractive wall around my property. How else can I keep out wayward sheep determined to feast on my begonias and hollyhocks? If this is a portmanteau refuge, give me seedy suburbia anytime."

Clearly, we have much to do in the name of homely integration.

NOVEMBER, 1984

Norfolk has plenty of raw material for writers. I'm thinking seriously about a local follow-up to put "Dallas" in the shade. Do you think "Sea Palling" has the right sort of ring? I'll eat my stetson if the networks turn it down.

It was the sight of fourteen-ton vibrator vehicles trying to sneak past without signing autographs that started it all. They were called up to help in a major survey that could knock a few more holes in Norfolk's reputation as the place for rural backwaters. A geophysical firm based in Kent hopped over to take seismic readings over a triangular section from Great Yarmouth to Sea Palling and on to Brundall. The target – a major oil or gas trend coming inland from fields in the North Sea.

No panic yet, though, because it'll take a year to sift through the survey results. Any promising signs, and the J.R. bandwagon could roll again next autumn. One little warning to Norfolk landowners nursing dreams of striking it rich and building their own skyscraper overlooking Halvergate Marshes. All the mineral rights in this country belong to the Crown. Americans have more incentives to go digging and so inspire those wonderful oil-operas on the box.

Sorry you may have to wait for a barrel or two of laughs, Sea Palling, but we have had these sort of promises before. What do you mean, you don't care if I never turn up for the auditions?

JANUARY, 1985

On the reasonable assumption that any resolutions I make for myself could well be torn to shreds by the end of January, I've decided to offer a few guidelines for those who'd like to see Norfolk through 1985 without too many more self-inflicted wounds.

These suggestions do emanate from a parochial pulpit, but my texts for the next twelve months are based on a genuine belief that we've reached a point where homespun thinking must push aside headlong acceptance of anything marked "progress".

I'm fed up with Norfolk natives yielding good ground – and then asking where its gone. I'm fed up with commercial interests mocking our lack of ambition and drive – and then setting up shop to help us out of a muddle.

I'm fed up with patronising taps on the head from newcomers who think our mode of life is so wonderful they're quite happy to stand back and watch. I'm sick and tired of anyone who wants Norfolk to be a boring photostat of everywhere else.

With these little gripes in mind, I've compiled Ten Rustic Commandments that might help us come to terms with a Norfolk that can continue to change without surrendering its complete identity.

THOU SHALT NOT automatically assume dual-carriageways and other major developments will make the county a better place in which to live. (Bicycle rally from the old blacksmith's shop to a supermarket of your choice is best means of protest. Pickets at check-out to be orderly.)

THOU SHALT NOT stand by and watch your local pub turn into an amusement arcade with food and plastic fittings. (Demand exclusive corner for dominoes and clog dancing. Feed washers into any machine, and take own sandwiches wrapped in newspaper.)

THOU SHALT NOT support any politician who hasn't lived in the county for at least five years. (Heckle at the hustings in broad Norfolk, ask for full details of the 1958–59 Cup Run and demand dialect lessons in any village school their policies might leave.)

THOU SHALT NOT accept radical changes at seaside resorts where the "old-fashioned" flavour is strongest. (Organise donkey rides along the front, and make sandcastles for the rest of the day if you fall off. "Kiss-Me-Slow" hats are optional.)

THOU SHALT NOT give misleading instructions if holidaymakers ask the way. (Unless they laugh at the way you talk.)

THOU SHALT complain to anyone who'll listen if something you think is important comes under threat. (Schools, pubs, churches, shops, buses, trains, hedges, woods . . . or the effect of military exercises on your ferrets' breeding habits.)

◀ *Land Army girl with the agricultural troops.* (Picture provided by Brian Hedge.)

Girls and boys can be useful at harvest time.

    (Picture by Clifford Temple.)

THOU SHALT welcome all newcomers to the area with a cup of tea and a friendly mardle before asking if they mean to take part in the local community life. (If your overtures are ignored, propose them as village hall committee members or school managers so other locals can call round and drink their tea.)

THOU SHALT sing the praises of Norfolk at every opportunity. (This does not mean constantly wallowing in nostalgia, calling your house "Dun Troshin" and going to work on a honeycart. Cadge a lift with a new neighbour where possible.)

THOU SHALT support your local garden fete and as many other functions as possible. (Sending a jar of jam for the home produce stall and a buttonhole for the vicar is not enough. He might ask who you are.)

THOU SHALT be wary of all who claim far-reaching alterations will affect them as much as you, for good or bad. (Tell them "dewing different" in Norfolk can mean leaving well alone.)

FEBRUARY, 1985

I see King's Lynn is earmarked for "Revolution", but it shouldn't be too brutal an affair. The town has been chosen as the setting for much of the work on a film of that name. Lynn waterfront, especially the port and Purfleet, will be made to look like New York in the 18th century, and there'll be chances for dozens of local people to become film extras. The film-makers cast an eye over towns up and down Britain before settling on Lynn.

Stand by for flocks of American tourists anxious to see where the epic was made ... and more Norfolk locations picked out for the big celluloid treatment.

"Gone With The Wind" on Halvergate Marshes in Glorious Broadlandscope ... "Bad Day At North Creake" and "Wells Fargo" as a teasing Western double bill ... "One Flew Over The Turkey's Nest" set in bewtiful Great Witchingham ... "Hingham High", Norfolk's first spaghetti Eastern ... "Carrowsell", the musical that's hotter than mustard ... "Yanks", the story of a Norfolk aerodrome ... "Great Oakspectations", the wonderful world of Dickens in Thetford Chase...

Make your own up, give Hollywood a call and earn a few dollars more for the Norfolk Budget.

MARCH, 1985

March can be a spiteful month, mocking dreams of another cricket season, another summer, another tan to turn them green with envy at the office. It can build up anticipation one day, with that sense of peaceful power in the world of reawakening nature, and then conjure stinging winds and sudden snowflakes out of nowhere to remind us winter hasn't yet disappeared over the headlands.

My friend who makes up old Norfolk sayings and verses has been known to compare this month to a fickle female, possibly out of memories of some ill-fated peccadillo when his buskins were all shiny and new, and the sap was a' rising. He puts it thus:

> March? Thass lyke a mawther wot giv yer a
>   sunny smyle,
> But yewre still serspishus sheez a cold'un orl
>   the whyle!

To help him forget, and perhaps look more kindly on the fairer sex, I've pointed him towards lines from George Meredith's "Invitation to the Country":

> *Now 'tis Spring on wood and wold,*
> *Early Spring that shivers with cold,*
> *But gladdens, and gathers, day by day,*
> *A lovelier hue, a warmer ray.*

APRIL, 1985

Easter brings the holiday mood to life after a winter of sizing up all the brochures and their tantalising images. The big trips to far-off climes have to wait a while, but there'll be plenty of rehearsing in Norfolk during the next few weeks.

I suspect many locals nip down to the coast for a spot of fresh air and fun before the visitors move in. In some cases, there are the first family reunions since Christmas. "Let's go and see Granny, and then we'll all go to Cromer for the afternoon." A traditional ruffling of the feathers after long, cold months relying on television for entertainment. Happy release from the fireside where the holiday dreams dance in the flames.

North Norfolk remains a refuge for those who prefer their breaks at a more gentle pace, although certain pressures are being exerted to bring the area more into line with other parts where the holiday trade is important.

I think that's a big mistake. But I have no vested interest in the tourist industry, and I'll confess immediately to being outlandishly old-fashioned. An incurable romantic, if you like, although harsh realities have been known to smack dreamers like me square between the eyes.

During our January hibernation, BBC Television did their best to arouse curiosity on a national scale when it comes to the largely-unsullied delights of North Norfolk. "Poppyland" became a magnet for the arty London set just over a century ago when writer Clement Scott gave it the full "paradise" treatment. But it wasn't long before he was wishing he'd kept the discovery to himself to avoid it becoming "Bungalow Land".

The irony remains. If pushing a quiet unspoilt area into the spotlight with effective salesmanship is effective, too many people respond – and so destroy

Echo from Great Yarmouth's past. (Picture provided by Brian Hedge.)

the very commodity they've come to savour. Perhaps it's downright selfish, but if you find your "Poppyland", there's something to be said for enjoying it – and keeping quiet.

JULY, 1985

It's too easy to be nostalgic for a past you didn't have to live through. I wasn't about, but I know life on our local farms in the 19th century was ruled by poverty and hard graft. They toiled to make much of their little, especially when it came to the corn harvest. For firm evidence, just turn to the work of country writers like John Clare, Robert Bloomfield, George Crabbe and Matilda Betham-Edwards. As much about muck and sweat as the swain under cloudless skies.

For all that, there's an obvious yearning for a more recent past as the combines wait impatiently to start chewing up the golden acres. They're big, noisy and efficient, and an affront even to some of the operators who took childhood sips of Cider with Rosie.

Giant Hoovers, sweeping and cleaning. Headlights turn it all into some grotesque ballet of the countryside when the sun's gone down. The coronation of the year has no lingering majesty. Harvest has been stripped of its ceremonial robes.

We can no more turn back the clock than order a record yield. But I think it's worth asking what we miss most out of all the items now on display in rural life museums. The scythe and the sickle, memorable for the simplicity and adequacy of their design. The binder and elevator, chugging partners on the stack-making scene.

Piling the sheaves into stooks. The glorious art of thatching. Horses and jugs of beer. Stick-waving lads chasing rabbits. The Harvest Supper or Horkey. A feast and frolic to bind farmers and workers in whole-hearted thanks for another harvest safely gathered in.

The rural spirit being fed along with the body. The Lord of the Harvest proposing the toast: "Here's health unto our master, the founder of the feast." Ale and tobacco all round. Barriers down, togetherness scything through the usual self-conciousness. But hold you hard, ole partners!

My friend who makes up old Norfolk sayings, and who claims to have reaped much more than he's sown, has a timely warning against a full-time return to the traditional Harvest Horkey. He points to the old Norfolk custom of Ten Pounding as a good example of what is best left over the headlands. Any worker caught breaking the harvest rules was subjected to a swift court-martial. If he was found guilty, he was instantly seized and thrown down flat on his back.

My report from the rustic ringside continues: "Some of the party keep his head down, and confine his arms, while others turn up his legs in the air so as to exhibit his posteriors. The person who is to inflict the punishment then takes a shoe, and with the heel of it (studded as it usually is with hob nails) gives him the prescribed number of blows upon his breech, according to the sentence.

"The rest of the party sit by, with their hats off, to see that the executioner does his duty; and if he fails in this, he undergoes the same punishment. It sometimes happens that, from the prevailing use of high-lows (ankle boots), a shoe is not to be found among the company. In this case, the hardest and heaviest hand of the reap is selected for the instrument of correction, and, when it is laid on with a hearty good will, it is not inferior to the shoe."

Do you give in? Had enough of the good old days of trial and stubble? Instant rough justice at the Norfolk Harvest Horkey hardly qualifies as genuine nostalgia.

And yet the modern mechanised charge across the fields goes against the grain. Glean the middle ground of your own memories, and sort out the wheat from the chaff before the threshing tackle gets here.

AUGUST, 1985

I was fascinated to learn that the farmers' survival kit after a nuclear attack will be made up of polythene sheets, a bucket of dirt and an ample supply of straw bales.

Whitehall buffs are urging farmers to fill cowshed attics with soil, bring in as many animals as possible and protect the rest from radiation fall-out in straw bale pens covered with polythene. Water supplies must also be protected from contamination and covered with polythene.

Farmers will be alerted to a nuclear attack by maroon, gong or whistle. I was chatting about this to a Norfolk son of the soil the other day. Here's just hoping no-one starts strolling over local fields pretending to be a ship in distress, a diligent butler or a football referee.

Mind you, he can remember being put on his guard during the last war by that famous leaflet issued by the Ministry of Information in co-operation with the War Office and the Ministry of Home Security. *If The Invader Comes* was packed with useful tips like: "Do not give any German anything. Do not tell him anything. Hide your food and your bicycles. Hide your maps. See that the enemy gets no petrol."

And let me paraphrase a sharp reminder that wouldn't go amiss these days. The only thing that gets thicker as you spread it is ... rumour.

OCTOBER, 1985

An illustrious band of scholars have forecast the demise of the Norfolk dialect since that bright lad Sir Thomas Browne became the first person to take notice in writing that the county had one.

That was in the latter part of the 17th century. Since then, several others have collected examples for general consumption, coated them in obvious affection – and then warned that it was only a matter of time before they disappeared. Some words and expressions have gone, along with the ways of life that inspired them. But there remains a healthy base for natives and newcomers to savour. Remember, Sir Thomas Browne was a Londoner.

He listed twenty-six examples of "words of no general reception in England but of common use in Norfolk". A few were already obsolete by the time Robert Forby got cracking with his Vocabulary of East Anglia over a century later.

He seemed convinced he was recording a dialect bound to die out with advances in education and better communications. Harry Cozens-Hardy own-ed up to a similar feeling when he pieced together his Broad Norfolk booklet in 1893, a collection of letters to the *Eastern Daily Press* featuring the dialect. He pointed to the Board Schools as the main reason for his prophecy that the vernacular would wither within the next generation.

Well, I'm sure Harry won't put his parts on or kick up a duller if I suggest he takes a little humble pie with his heavenly wittles. He wasn't the first to be proved wrong – and he won't be the last.

Perhaps you have to listen very carefully to catch an old-timer exclaim "Lork-a-masser!" instead of "Lord have mercy", but you can still get a funny mobbin if you stand round like a duzzy mawkin when a good tidy lot are working hard.

NOVEMBER, 1985

How pleasing to note that young people in this area are the most romantic in the country, at least from a Post Office point of view. Seventeen per cent of them admitted to writing a love letter in the past three months, compared to only two per cent in the North. Boys, apparently, are twice as likely to write to their loved ones as girls.

I recall a few "SWALK" efforts hastily composed under the desk lid at school, but the Post Office didn't come into play. A couple of fluffy peardrops would usually encourage a sister, or another girl of plainer qualities, to deliver the missive to the object of all those pent-up desires. Such red-faced shame if the letter was intercepted by some horrible bully-boy, or a teacher fascinated by such a poetic turn of phrase.

"Mete me neer the raylings at playtime and I'll love you forever." Did any of those little rosebuds hang on to those scribbled outpourings? Has Eamonn Andrews got them all in case he comes to Norfolk with the famous red book?

In any event, we should be delighted that our successors are still getting a tingle out of the old quill and parchment. I thought most of today's romances were conducted by telephone.

The Magpie

As a "media person" since 1962, I've had little choice but to develop the magpie instinct. In fact, the process began while I was at school, collecting yarns from other boys anxious to break the monotony of detention. Some of those stories still come in handy for after-dinner speeches.

Cuttings yellow with age and pictures curling at the edges are the legacy of seventeen years of news-gathering on the local beat. Thetford trying to come to terms with overspill from London. Dereham anxious to find the right balance between traditional virtues and more development. Great Yarmouth striving to make the most of industry and entertainment.

Perhaps the changes and the challenges didn't affect me so much when I moved to Norwich to concentrate on writing about sport for a living. Travelling with the Canaries to exotic spots like Derby, Stoke, Leeds, Bolton and Watford tended to exaggerate Norfolk's natural beauties!

In any event, my switch to the local wireless has reawakened interest in local issues – and reinforced the magpie urge. Letters and tapes have piled up alongside the newspaper mementoes. The bulk of them reflect deep concern at the way Norfolk is being asked to square up to radical changes.

The growth of suburbia around Norwich, declining numbers in agriculture and the big push to attract more tourists are the obvious starters. But there are more subtle forces at work at a time when standing still is regarded as a sin – and looking over your shoulder is just so much sentimental hogwash.

There seems to be no indigenous middle class in the county, and that's why many of the important decisions are taken by people who have moved in. Planners and other council officials who started their careers elsewhere will argue that they can make important comparisons with other areas, and bring a much-needed sense of perspective. We natives demand they pay more attention to our traditions, and listen to local comparisons they cannot make.

After all, that's the first rule to be observed by any tactful newcomer to any small community. When in Tittleshall or Topcroft ... don't try to impose a different set of values on the natives if they're quite happy with the ones they've got. If changes must come, let them be natural.

Closing so many of our village schools not only raises hackles in the communities concerned – despite all the economic arguments – but also undermines those familiar claims about the need for long-term thinking. In one breath we're told smaller villages can absorb reasonable amounts of development without destroying the essential character. The next breath blows away the school – and defies young families to move in and confirm the children as mini-commuters.

Thankfully, numerous brave battles have been waged in the name of preserving an essential strand in the tapestry of Norfolk rural life, and there'll be many more full-blooded rounds before the end of the century. One of the most effective jabs to the solar plexus is to ask members of education authorities how many of their children attended, or are attending, village schools.

Enter the magpie with a couple of handy cuttings from the Norfolk nest. The first, from *The Norfolk Magazine* of July, 1948, stresses the size of the divide between some newcomers and natives. The second, from my own *Dereham and Fakenham Times* notebook of 1963, highlights growing concern for the future of village life.

That magazine article by H. J. Harcourt, entitled "Viking or Bor?" could have been written last week, and I suspect it'll be just as topical twenty years from now:

"Strangers who come into our midst are inclined to treat us either with benevolent condescension or with undisguised superciliousness – and then expect us to acclaim them as saviours and the harbingers of civilisation.

"H. V. Morton, in his book, *In Search of England*, describes Norfolk as 'the most suspicious county in England', and then gives an explanation. He says the East Anglians were constantly invaded throughout ancient history, and bitter experience has taught them to divide humanity into 'vikings' and 'bors', the latter being loosely translated as 'neighbours'.

"The modern viking can best be described as the smart-alec, the laddie who comes along to tell us how it should all be done. These smart-alecs have several lines, although they all approximate to the same pattern. They tell us Norfolk is flat, dull, uninteresting; our particular town or village is one-eyed, one-horse, back of beyond; we are provincial, parochial, bovine. Where they come from, of course, things are different – and better.

"They come from the industrial centres of Lancashire, Yorkshire and the Midlands, where they have the advantage of constant smoke and rain, where everything is grey and grim and dour and ugly. Or they have spent all their lives in a mountainous district, with their vision always obscured by that same slab-sided mountain.

"Or they come from London, where they say they lived the 'full life' – catching the seven-something from Dormitoria or Suburbia to London, and the six-something back again! But in every case we must congratulate them on having had the good sense to shake the dust of these places from their shoes by moving to Norfolk.

"What we object to is being treated as congenital idiots because it was not necessary for us to travel to obtain the pleasures of living here."

Remember, all that was written nearly forty years ago when the numbers of folk discovering the delights of Norfolk, either as settlers or holidaymakers, were far lower than they are today. The bigger the influx – the louder the debate.

My cutting from 1963 concerns a one-day school at Dereham when Norman and Elizabeth Tillett, W.E.A. tutors in Norfolk and lecturers to the Civic Trust, warned that our village life was almost certain to be transformed within ten years. The prospect of being forced to marry industry to rural life was the key topic.

Mrs Tillett said the sentimental attachment to the word "village" was very strong in Norfolk. It conjured up a picture of a closely-knit community clustered round the green or church – a picture which was sometimes true.

Overspill would undoubtedly affect these as much as the towns, but here the problem would be more of a sociological one for "a community spirit within the village is something that cannot be forced". She said there were already signs of the "two-dimensional village" – those who worked in and around the village and the commuters who worked in the cities and towns.

She suggested the formation of a village society to deal with the inevitable problem of fostering a community spirit between the newcomers and those who resented their appearance on the village scene – otherwise the problem would be that of a community split asunder.

Mrs Tillett said she was convinced that planners and surveyors did not know enough about the countryside. Their training was far too concerned with towns and cities. The haphazard "plonking" of houses in the countryside was evidence to support this.

Her husband, a former Lord Mayor of Norwich, and city councillor, said the expected influx of population into the county would make the current over-spill programme look like chicken feed. One of the things we didn't want was "the nasty mixture of part village, part town" which we had at the moment. An avoidance of a "universal suburbia" was most necessary. The town and country represented two ways of life and it was wrong to mix them indiscriminately.

Warnings from 1963. How many fell on stony ground? Or even concrete? A more recent visit from my magpie brought a major speech by a Norfolk MP in June, 1986. Growing prosperity and popularity could turn the county into a dormitory sprawl on a carpet of concrete, said South Norfolk MP John MacGregor. How many people could be absorbed without destroying Norfolk's character?

"If Norfolk is to remain an attractive place to live and work, it has to get right vital issues such as roads, agriculture and business structure." With more road improvements and electrification of the rail line to London, South Norfolk was presented with the challenge of avoiding "going the way of some Home Counties, with their congestion, their choked byroads and their commuter mentality.

"What should the next stage be? We must have some bypasses, yes, to keep the towns and villages worst affected still attractive places to live in. But we must avoid making Norfolk, particularly south of Norwich, a carpet of concrete."

That speech was the signal for the latest "Great Debate" on our county's future. The more cynical suggest we're due for another one as soon as the concrete has settled. After all, the cry of "it'll bring jobs" still carries more weight than the most heartfelt: "but it'll spoil the look of the place".

I don't have to worry about votes. I'm not an employer. I don't make big decisions in council chambers. But there are certain responsibilities, shared with all Norfolk natives or newcomers who care enough to recognise them. And I do have the magpie to remind me.

If it rain or if it snow
Keep a-goin',
If it hail or if it blow
Keep a-goin',
Tent no use t' set an' whine
Cors a fish ent on yar line,
Bait yar hook an' keep a-tryin',
Keep a-goin'.

(From a Victorian book of *Norfolk Gleanings*.)

A Norfolk Stocking

He was alone. He bolted the door, brushed the crumbs from the newspaper spread over the table, and watched a few pale trimmings tremble above the hearth.

Up the twisting stairs to a bedroom where he had trodden with such stealth many years ago when Christmas Eve meant two contrasting worlds, and he loved both of them. The village pub and its raucous celebrations. Home and the furtive fumblings at the foot of the bed where the children might be pretending to be asleep.

Both these worlds had gone. It was cheating to think memories could bring them back. They'd been kind in their way and offered to take him to a restaurant. They'd been secretly relieved when he turned down the invitation, but their secrets were wasted on him. He'd heard them chattering while washing up the other Sunday...

Sleep came easy. Christmas Day came quickly. He made the bed before pulling back the curtains and peering across the fields. "Nut tew menny slidjemarks, ole partner. Wunder if he know sum onnus still live heer!" The chuckle followed him to the fireplace where a log was still smouldering.

The second cup of tea was on its way out when a knock on the door reminded him that he was still locked in. No-one there as he breathed in the morning. Just an old water-boot lolling against the rain tub, and he would have ignored that but for the holly-berry paper poking out of the top.

There was a crumpled note pinned to the inside of the boot, and he recognised the writing as soon as he'd torn it out. The second chuckle of the day would echo right through to the evening.

"Thass ryte sorft us bein on owr own terdayer orl daze. Heers a pudden we kin boyl up an a dropper suffin ter wosh it down. Praps yewre got wunner tew things in th'old pantry. Iyll be rownd sewn arter Iyre cleered up an fed the dawg. Bet yer carnt wearte."

She arrived an hour later, just as a fresh log was crackling and the kettle singing.

OLD GEORGE'S SARMON

I arnt much of a religious chap. That fare a
    proper mix up ter me.
Some on 'em say one thing An' some on 'em say
    another
Till you don't know whu ter believe. Our wicar
    he's a rare nice feller,
He's what they call a Master-er-Arts. He earnt
    none the wuss for that,
But I don't allus know what he's talkin' about.
    Some o' the chapel folks arnt much better,
They ha' got wery respectable now-a-days. We
    had one here th' other Sunday.
He used some master gret long wahds What
    dint mean nothin' tu most on us,
Mind ye, bor, he wornt no fule. But he dint fare
    to *git* nowhere.

The best sarmon iver I recollect I heerd on a
    fourteen acre fild.
Thass werry near fifty year ago. I was ondly a
    boy at the time,
But I remember as if that was yistiddy. We
    were at wark a drillin' o' wheat.
I was a leadin' the old fore hoss An' that was a
    rainin' good tidily.
Tom say, "In with a slop, a heavier crop." But I
    was werry near wet tru.
I said some wahds I owt not to ha' said. Our old
    patner George he say to me.
"Jest you moderate yar language." I say, "Ha'
    you swallerd a dictionary?
"I know you're a bit of a preacher But where's
    yar religion got you
"You're ondly a lab'rer like the rest on 'em
    Gitting yer ten bob a week."

Old George was a master one for Scripture
    Though he never went to school in his life.
He say, "Harrer, bor, don't be silly bold, An'
    don't never say '*ondly* a labourer'.
"I ha' worked on this here fild, Wheat,
    mangolds, barley and hay
"For werry near forty year, But th' Almighty
    He ha' warked on it
"Since the werry beginning of creation, An'
    whether you know it or no
"He's warkin' with us ter day. Let us du our job
    properly
"Else all His wark 'll be wasted, Don't never say
    'ondly a labourer',
"We are labourers together with God."

No, I arnt a werry religious chap But I
    remember old George's sarmon
Though thass werry near fifty year ago, An,
    that du fare to make a difference.
                                          C.L.S.

One of the most compelling hymns of praise composed for Norfolk came from
the pen of Canon F. C. Oakley. He was Rector of Necton from 1926 until 1945.
Then he left for missionary work in Antigua, where he died in 1953.

A former curate of St. Peter Mancroft and Wymondham, he was Classics
master at Norwich School, Rural Dean of Swaffham and Honorary Canon of
Norwich Cathedral. In 1941, he became editor of the *Diocesan Gazette*.

Canon Oakley's verses about Norfolk are regulation issue for exiles thinking of home . . . .

NORFOLK

God drew the map of England,
He planted hill and wood,
He looked on stream and headland,
And saw that it was good.

Pushed far into a corner,
He left a fair domain,
Heath, down, and fen, and ploughland,
Rich pasturage and grain.

It's on the road to Nowhere
Travellers pass it by,
Nobody comes to Norfolk,
Without a reason why.

Nobody sings of Norfolk,
Though many bards there be
To honour glorious Devon,
Or Sussex by the sea.

When God made Norfolk County,
He said they'd love her well
Who, patient in her wooing
Surrendered to her spell.

Slowly she charms, how slowly,
But once the spell is cast
By Norfolk on her lovers,
She holds them to the last.

Norfolk's a stately lady
She'll keep aloof for years,
"Furriners" she despises,
She's scornful of the "Sheers".

But they'll not hold her fickle
Who once her true love win,
From Brancaster to Thetford,
From Caister to King's Lynn.

We're slow of speech in Norfolk,
Perhaps a thought too slow,
And only when we're cornered
We'll answer "Yes" or "No".

Our Fathers taught us caution
They learned with moil and pain
That every Precious stranger
Might be a thieving Dane.

The sturdy Norfolk yeoman
To guard their rights are set
As well befits the children
Of men who followed Kett.

Yet Norfolk men are loyal,
Without deceit or sham,
Ask, if you think it doubtful
The "Squire of Sandringham".

Devon may boast her sailors,
But Norfolk holds the claim
To lead all other counties
By right of Nelson's name.

And mark in France and Flanders,
And far beyond the waves,
The thousand wooden crosses
Guarding our Norfolk graves.

When God made Norfolk County
He showed this perfect art,
Within her fair, proud body
He hid a golden heart.

So come and live in Norfolk
Bide, till her spell is cast,
Then, once you've learned to love her,
You'll love her to the last.

Transparency provided by Alan Tickle. ▶

Dear God,

Yew give us a rare nyce plearse ter live in, ole partner, an weed lyke ter arsk fer yar help ter keep it that way. That ent allus eezy ter leave things aloon when yewre arter a bit moor, but praps yew kin larn us nut ter be tew greedy.

Yew know we wotter dew ryte by orl them wot cum an live longer us, but dew yew put them streart bowt wunner tew things.

We carnt chearnj fer searke onnit, an that ent no cop them tryin ter mearke us.

No moor kin we sit an howld owr slarver whyle they hevver go tharselves, and say: "Theeryar – thass how that orter be." Whyle yewre bowt it, jist yew hevver wad longer orl them torists an tell 'em ter leeve the plearse way they fynd it. If thass datty up wun rood, that sewn spred t' nuther.

Bor Jesus lyked a bitter peese n' quwyet arter a good mardle. Thow we ent in his clarss that dunt dew ner harm ter try an foller his waze.

Kin yew see tew it we allus hev them backworters ter git yer wind an say thankyer? Weer gotter keep owr little bitter the wald suffin speshul.

Dew yew giv us a hand. Then we kin look arter it. Forever an ever . . .

Amen